C++

Addison-Wesley
Nitty Gritty

PROGRAMMING SERIES

C++

Till Jeske

ADDISON-WESLEY

An imprint of Pearson Education

Boston • San Francisco • New York • Toronto • Montreal • London • Munich
Paris • Madrid • Cape Town • Sydney • Tokyo • Singapore • Mexico City

PEARSON EDUCATION LIMITED

Head Office
Edinburgh Gate, Harlow, Essex CM20 2JE
Tel: +44 (0)1279 623623 Fax: +44 (0)1279 431059

London Office
128 Long Acre, London WC2E 9AN
Tel: +44 (0)20 7447 2000 Fax: +44 (0)20 7240 5771
Websites:
www.it-minds.com   www.aw.com/cseng

First published in Great Britain 2002
© Pearson Education Limited 2002

First Published in 2000 as *C++ Nitty-Gritty* by Addison Wesley, Verlag, Germany.

The rights of Till Jeske to be identified as Author of this Work have been asserted by him in accordance with the Copyright, Designs and Patents Act 1988.

Library of Congress Cataloging Publication Data
Applied for.

British Library Cataloging in Publication Data
A CIP catalogue record for this book can be obtained from the British Library.

ISBN 0-201-75879-2

10 9 8 7 6 5 4 3 2 1

Translated and typeset by Berlitz GlobalNET (UK) Ltd. of Luton, Bedfordshire.
Printed and bound in Great Britain by Biddles Ltd. of Guildford and King's Lynn.

The publishers' policy is to use paper manufactured from sustainable forests.

Contents

Preface

This book describes the ANSI C++ language in a succinct and concise form. A knowledge of C++ is not required in order to follow the explanations. They nevertheless lead in a steep learning curve from the introductory section to the critical aspects of the language which are outlined in the main section. Readers with experience of other programming languages will be familiar with this approach.

The main precept behind all the explanations is that of describing the individual language elements according to the way in which they are actually used, including their difficulties and particularities. In order to avoid interrupting a particular train of thought with syntax lists, the latter will be summarized in the reference section at the end of the book.

I would like to thank the revisers, Rüdiger Strasser, Ciske Busch, Martin Karmann and Dr. Michael Friedlinger for their support. My special thanks go to Dr. Bertram Pertzsch, whose valid comments helped bring the manuscript to fruition.

Part I

Start up!

Introduction

Let's forget theory for a moment and start straight away with an example.

```cpp
#include <iostream.h>
main () {
  cout << "C++ programming is fun." << endl;
}
```

This program displays the text "C++ programming is fun." Don't worry about the exact meaning of the various instructions. Just type them all into a word processor and save them under the name `example.cpp`. All the details will be explained later.

Next the program has to be translated. This means changing the more or less human-readable elements in the example into a combination of ones and zeros which the processor in your computer can understand. Only then can your computer execute the program. To translate or compile the program you need a compiler.

Compilers come in many different forms and vary in their ease of use. If you have Windows on your PC, a simple click on the appropriate icon will enable you to access an environment which will give you all you need for developing C++ software, including a tailor-made text-processing program, the actual compiler, and an integrated screen window in which the program is executed. In this particular case all you have to do is click on the compiler button and the program will be compiled. Any errors will be displayed in a separate window. You will then use the word processing facility in the development environment.

You are also catered for if your PC has a Linux operating system. Its compiler is concealed behind a rather austere `c++`, which you type in to the command line. To compile the example you input

```
c++ example.cpp.
```

The differences between the various compilers are only superficial as a rule. Many compilers, for example, use the standard endings `.cc`, `.C` or `.cxx` instead of `.cpp` for program files unless otherwise specified. The basic principle is the same in all cases. If in doubt, make use of the help facility incorporated in the compiler. Under Windows the Help button is a valuable source of information. Under Linux man cpp or man gpp will get you what you want.

Of course things may go wrong when you try out the compiler for the first time. If you do not use an integral development environment, for example, it may be that the c++ compiler cannot be found. Then you will have to find out in which directory it is located in your computer and include this directory in the environmental variable for executable files.

The compiler may also display an error message informing you that the file iostream.h cannot be found. This message refers to the first line in which a reference is made to the file in question. Try to find the folder containing the file and add its path to the path environmental variable. This variable may be called INCLUDE_PATH. You will find the exact name in the compiler manual.

Mistyping is another common cause of error. It is very easy to leave out quotation marks or a semicolon. Sometimes even a space in the wrong place can confuse the compiler. The messages generated by this error are often not very helpful. Therefore you must always check that the program you have typed in corresponds exactly with the example given in the book.

Once the program has been compiled you can execute it. In a graphical development environment all you have to do is click on the execute button. From the command line you call up the file (careful!) a.out. In either case you will see displayed

```
C++ programming is fun.
```

Welcome to the ranks of the C++ programmers! Technically speaking that was the most difficult step in the book, since we have not been able to give you much help with your particular development environment.

But wait a minute. We haven't finished with the specimen program yet. All the work is done by the third line which deals with the text output. Using cout << you can output a number of objects of data. For example, if you type in

```
cout << "My house number is " << 123 << "." << endl;
```

you will see displayed

```
My house number is 123.
```

You can string together as many objects – numerical or alphabetical – as you like using the double less-than sign <<. The instruction endl signifies *end line* and indicates that the line is complete. All command lines in C++ end with a semicolon.

The first line tells you which file `iostream.h` is needed to compile the `cout` instruction. The pointed brackets are deliberately left off the ending `.h`. Try leaving out the first line. The compiler will complain that it does not recognize `cout`.

That leaves just lines two and four, which form the corner-stone of a C++ program. The keyword `main` crops up in every program once and once only and marks the start of the main program. The main program is the part of the program which is executed first. The opening and closing curly brackets enclose all the commands which the program has to execute before completion.

The legacy of C

You may be an experienced C programmer interested in what new features C++ has to offer. Or you may want to start straight away with C++ without the detour via C. Either way you are faced with the common history of the two programming languages. C++ is an extension of C, a language which has stood the test of time for 25 years. In that time a number of new features have been added, the main effect of which has been to transform C++ into an object-oriented programming language, whereas C is purely procedural. What this means exactly is explained in Chapter 4. The differences are not so great, however, as to make it necessary to jettison all the knowledge and skills previously acquired. In fact most operating systems and many computer games are written in C, and they still run and run and run.

Therefore in conversion to C++ all of C's language elements have been retained. C++ is C writ large. Every C program can be compiled with a C++ compiler. To illustrate this here is a program which combines elements from both worlds.

```
#include <iostream.h>
#include <stdio.h>
main () {
  cout << "C++ programming is fun." << endl;
  printf ("C programming is too.\n");
}
```

The main program has been extended in the last line which, like the line above it, displays the text contained in the quotation marks. The newly added second line tells the compiler which file contains the new `printf` command. When compiled and executed the program displays

```
C++ programming is fun.
C programming is too.
```

Programmers experienced in C will recognize the syntax of the new lines. All other readers, however, will be asking: Why write the same command two completely different ways? The answer is that the old forms can be retained out of habit, but the new versions are generally more convenient to use. C++ has been provided with either additional functions or with instructions which have the same function but are much easier to use than their C equivalents. The latter is the case, as the C programmers among you will testify, when we output variables with cout.

From now on we shall opt for true C++ forms when there are equivalents in C. C is still of interest to us in areas where the notation of C and C++ is identical. These areas form the core of the two languages. For this reason we shall first explain the concepts which are common to C and C++. These concern variables, loops and conditional statements, and also functions and pointers. In order to enable you to immerse yourselves in the subject matter as quickly as possible, we shall not waste time at this point classifying the components of the language but simply introduce elements of the notation when they are first used. Thanks to the comprehensive reference section in Part 3 of the book you will not seek in vain for any information you need.

If you are a veteran programmer with experience in other languages, you can skip quickly through the next section. But you would do well to take note of the descriptions marked by a warning sign of the traps which lie in wait for you here and there. And from Chapter 3 onwards you too will find that the going begins to get tough, since it is at this point that the differences between C and C++ really begin to make themselves felt.

2.1 Variables, loops, conditional statements

Computer programs come into their own when you want to repeat a proven procedure automatically several times. This is done with the aid of loops. The next example displays the numbers 1 to 4.

```cpp
#include <iostream.h>
main () {
  // Initiate counter variable
  int count;
  count = 1;
  // Display variable in a loop and increment counter
  while (count < 5) {
    cout << "The counter variable is " << count << endl;
    count = count + 1;
  }
}
```

This program contains a number of new features. The first things to note are the descriptive statements in the body of the program. objects such as these from / / to the end of the line are comments which are ignored by the compiler. The sole purpose of comments is to make the program more readable.

The next thing to note is the line

```
int count;
```

in which the variable count is declared. This variable is of the type integer and is assigned the value 1 in the next line. Variables do not have to be declared at the start of a program as is the case in some other languages.

The keyword while causes the instructions in the curly brackets to be executed as long as the condition in the round brackets is fulfilled. As long as the variable count is less than five it is displayed and then increased by one. For the sake of clarity the code inside a loop is indented by a fixed number of places. This indentation has no other significance and you are free to deal with it as you wish.

The result of the program is

```
The counter variable is 1
The counter variable is 2
The counter variable is 3
The counter variable is 4
```

Many C programmers strive to make their programs as concise as possible. Opinions are divided about the value of this economical approach, but sooner or later you will come across programs like the following:

```
#include <iostream.h>
main () {
  // Display variable in a loop and increment counter
  for (int count = 1; count < 5; count++) {
    cout << "The counter variable is " << count << endl;
  }
}
```

This example does the same as the previous one. Instead of a while loop a for loop is used. The syntax of the for loop requires there to be an instruction in the round brackets, a condition and then another instruction, all three separated by semicolons. The first instruction sets the initial parameters for the loop. This can be any C++ instruction. The condition which follows is evaluated at each pass of the loop, and the loop continues to operate until the condition is no longer fulfilled. The final instruction is executed once after each pass. As with the while loop discussed above all the instructions between the curly brackets are executed at each pass.

This preference for the much shorter `for` loop is not the end of the matter, however. Two other shorthand forms have sneaked into the loop where they are not strictly speaking necessary. The line

```
int count = 1;
```

is a typical combination of variable declaration and initialization which in the first example of a loop was implemented in two separate lines.

The line

```
count++;
```

is the pride of every C guru. It means the same as

```
count = count + 1;
```

Let's assume that you want to display the numbers 0 to 20 in steps of four. You want to make sure that the results are right-aligned so that they are easy to see. For this you will need a conditional statement. If the result is a single-digit number, i.e. less than ten, you output an extra space. Otherwise it's the same code as before.

```
#include <iostream.h>
main () {
  // Loop
  for (int count = 0; count <= 20; count += 4) {
    // Case difference
    if (count < 10) {
    cout << "The counter variable is  " << count << endl;
  }
    else {
    cout << "The counter variable is " << count << endl;
  }
  }
}
```

You will notice a case difference within the loop beginning with `if`. When the condition in the round brackets has been fulfilled, the next block of code contained in the curly brackets is executed, otherwise the code following the `else` is implemented. The output is:

```
The counter variable is 0
The counter variable is 4
The counter variable is 8
The counter variable is 12
The counter variable is 16
The counter variable is 20
```

Loops are activated by the keywords `while` or `for`, conditions by `if` and `else`.

One detail in passing. The instruction

```
count += 4;
```

in the `for` loop stands for

```
count = count + 4;
```

The `else` branch of the `if` condition is optional. You do not have to include it and can make do with

```
if (...) { ... }
```

provided that no instruction is to be carried out in the latter case. You can even leave out the curly brackets if there is only a single statement associated with the condition.

```
if (x < 10)
  cout << "x is less than ten." << endl;
```

Watch out! Here lurks one of the most annoying aspects of C. Not only beginners fall for this trap. When you test for equality in an `if` statement, rather than for inequality as in the last example, you run the risk of confusing relational and assignment operators.

Correct is:

```
if (x == 10) { ... }
```

Incorrect is:

```
if (x = 10) { ... }
```

because C uses the single equals sign for assignment purposes, and in this case x is being assigned a value of 10. The compiler interprets the result as a condition, which to crown it all has been fulfilled. This is because the compiler converts conditions into integer values. A zero signifies false, and all other values, including 10, signify true.

> **Warning** The symbols for assignment = and relation == are easily confused, and the resulting errors are all the more difficult to find.

2.2 Variables under the microscope

Besides the variable type `int` for integers there are other types for floating point numbers and characters.

```
double pi = 3.1415926;
char c = 'A';
```

In addition other types are available for higher value integers and floating point numbers, unsigned if necessary.

```
long int longInteger = -300000000;
unsigned int unsignedInteger = 456789;
unsigned double unsignedfloat = 1.55;
```

You will find the exact range of values of these types and of other similar types in the reference section at the end of the book. All you need to know at this juncture is that there are different types of variable and that they are kept strictly distinct by the compiler. If an assignment such as

```
long int = pi;
```

is made, the compiler will issue a warning, since it is not clear how the fractional digits of the floating point number are to be treated when assigned to an integer. This seems unnecessarily restrictive at first sight. After all the compiler could simply discard the fractional digits. However the user is spared the trouble of lengthy searches for content errors by the compiler's automatic strict type-testing. Imagine what would happen if the compiler simply discarded the fractional digits in an assignment. How long would you have to search in a large program to find the line where accuracy, once present, has been forfeited?

In situations where the user consciously intends to make this kind of assignment it is possible to force an expression to be of a specific type. The assignment is labeled a typecast or simply a cast and marked by entering the required type in brackets in front of the variable which is to be assigned. On the next line a cast statement is used to assign the floating point value defined above of `pi` to an integer.

```
int approxPi = (int)pi;
```

You can see that the approximation 3 for pi can have undesired effects if you are drawing circles. Explicit casts should be used sparingly or not at all.

Since we are dealing with pi, it seems reasonable to treat it as it really is, i.e. a constant. It makes a lot of sense to define a variable named `pi` so that we do not have to ascribe a value of 3.14... in each part of the program in which pi is used. Since this value remains unchanged for all eternity, we should identify it as invariable by preceding it with the keyword `const`.

```
const double pi = 3.1415926;
```

Now the variable `pi` is safe from false assignments. Never again will you be tempted anywhere in your program to write

```
pi = 4;
```

The compiler prevents variables defined as `const` from being assigned a value. An exception is of course the very first assignment when the variable is declared.

When using variable names you should distinguish between capitals and lower case letters, because the compiler does it too. The variable `numberofhits` is different from the variables `NumberofHits` and `NUMBEROFHITS`. If you assign a value to one of them, the other remains unchanged. If you declare one of them, the other remains undeclared.

Warning Capital letters and lower case letters are not interchangeable in variable names.

This brings us to the problem of variables with the same name and their validity. Clearly two variables with the same name cannot be declared consecutively. Which value would be output in the third of the following lines?

```
int num = 13;
int num = 100;  // Will not compile!
cout << "num has a value of " << count<< endl;
```

The compiler immediately rejects the second line. More problematical is the situation in the next example, which the compiler will in fact compile.

```
#include <iostream.h>
main () {
  int i = 3;
  cout << "i has a value of " << i << endl;
  {
    int i = 5;
    cout << "i has a value of " << i << endl;
  }
  cout << "i has a value of " << i << endl;
}
```

The variable `i` is defined in the body of the main program surrounded by curly brackets. It has a value of 3. Within the main program a second block is defined which is also surrounded by curly brackets. You will be familiar with the principle of nested blocks of code from loops and conditional statements. A block can also stand alone, however, as here. This highlights the true significance of the block. It identifies the area within which all the variables defined in it are valid. At the same time it shields the variables defined in it from conflicting with variables of the same name defined outside the block. This explains why the two definitions of the much-used variable i do not clash. Outside the block the variable defined there is meant when i is used. Inside the block the variable defined inside is meant. The program's output is therefore:

```
i has a value of 3
i has a value of 5
i has a value of 3
```

Not only do the closing brackets of a block have the effect of rendering the variables defined in the block subsequently invisible, but they also displace them physically. This may sound like a philosophical point, but in practice it means that the memory location which was previously occupied by a variable in the block has again become available.

Tip Variables are only visible in their surrounding block and must be uniquely named in that block.

The properties of program blocks quoted in the example apply equally to all other forms of program block. It makes no difference which keyword initializes the block, be it for, while or if or any other keyword hitherto not described.

To conclude this section here is an example of one of the few objects of C++ notation which are less useful than their C equivalents. A variable can be simultaneously declared and initialized both by

```
int num = 13;
```

and by

```
int num(13);
```

Both lines are absolute equivalents. In the case of basic variable types such as int the second variant has not caught on. As soon as we start to define types of our own, however, we shall find that it is used more frequently. Then you will do well to recall coming across it as a possible variant.

When you have read this chapter you will have made an acquaintance with the basic vocabulary of the C and C++ languages. This means you could in principle write any complex program you like by squeezing all the instructions between the curly brackets of the main program. You will soon realize that this is not feasible the minute you have lost your way in a hundred line program.

Since the sixties this effect has been known as the software crisis. The next time your favorite word processor crashes due to a protection error you will realize that thirty years later the crisis is still not quite over. Fortunately, however, ways have been developed of helping humans to cope with ever increasing processor and memory capacities.

An early move in this direction was the combination of frequently used pieces of code into a single entity with a label. Such an entity is called function. Once you have declared a function you can call it up by its name from any part of your program.

2.3.1   Example of a function

Here is an example of a function which displays a right-aligned number. Notice first of all how it is defined. The actual code will be discussed later.

```
#include <iostream.h>
// Definition of the function numDisplay
void numDisplay (int num) {
  int copy = num;
  for (int col=0; col<10; col++) {
    if (copy < 1) {
      cout << " " ;
    }
    copy = copy/10;
  }
  cout << num << endl;
}
// Main program
main () {
  // Call up function numDisplay
  numDisplay (199);
  numDisplay (3);
  numDisplay (4984);
}
```

Unlike some other languages C++ has no keyword "function" to indicate that a function is being declared. Instead the declaration line has the following format:

```
void numDisplay (int num)
```

The brackets contain the parameters of the function with its type. The significance of the parameter num is revealed in the main program, in which the same function is called up with different numerical values. The output is:

```
      199
        3
     4984
```

The function, which is surrounded by curly brackets, contains a copy of the output variable. By dividing this variable copy by 10 we gradually reduce it by one integer place. As soon as copy is less than 1 we have to equalize the missing places by outputting blank characters. Finally the actual number is displayed.

Tip Functions are named sections of code which can be called up via their name.

By using a function you will save yourself the trouble of having to write code for right-aligned output for each and every number displayed. This not only reduces the amount of typing you have to do, but also helps you to avoid errors which might occur if you decide to alter the code. In short, your program will be easier to maintain.

2.3.2 Return values

You may have wondered about the significance of the word void in front of the function name in the section where the function is declared. If you figured that it must represent the type of function by analogy with a variable declaration, you were quite right. In fact this is a return type function. The expression void indicates that a function, like that in the example, does not return a value to the calling program.

A function which returns a value might look like this:

```
int minimum (int num1, int num2) {
  if (num1 < num2) {
    return num1;
  } else {
    return num2;
  }
}
```

In the main program it can be used in the same way as a value of the type `int`.

```
main () {
   int x = 25;
   int y = 13;
   cout << "The minimum of " << x << " and "
        << y << " is " << minimum (x, y)
        << "." << endl;
}
```

The expected output is

```
The minimum of 25 and 13 is 13.
```

The keyword used in the program code for the function transfers the `return` value to the calling program. The return variable – here `num1` and `num2` – must be identical to the type of return variable in the function declaration. Both are integers in the example. However, instead of a variable the statement `return` can be used to return a value directly.

```
return 5;
```

A further side effect of the `return` statement is to terminate the function irrespective of how many lines come after the `return`. For this reason it makes sense to have a `return` statement in functions which do not return a value. `return` is then used with no following value. Functions without a return value, however, must not use a `return` statement.

A function gives a return value to the calling program via the keyword `return` and then terminates.

In the last example out of necessity, we have introduced you to another new feature of C++ programming which has only partly to do with the typesetting of the book. The statement in the main program which outputs the minimum takes up more than one line. This presents no problem for the compiler provided that variable names, keywords and text in quotation marks are not split up.

2.3.3   Passing parameters means copying

Finally we should like to examine by way of a simple example the relationship between the parameters within a function and the variables which are transferred to the function. For this purpose we have written a function for exchanging the two transferred variables.

```
void exchange (int num1, int num2) {
  int temp = num1; // Temporary variable
  num1 = num2;
  num2 = temp;
}
```

A program with the lines

```
int a = 13;
int b = 5;
cout << a << " " << b << endl;
exchange (a, b);
cout << a << " " << b << endl;
```

gives the following peculiar output

```
13  5
13  5
```

There is no question of an exchange having occurred here. What has happened? The variables a and b have been transferred to the parameters num1 and num2 in the exchange function. This does not mean, however, that num1 and a are identical, but merely that within the function a variable named num1 is available which has the same value as the variable a in the calling program. Or in other words num1 is a copy of a. Thus changing num1 has no effect on a.

This means that you can make any assignments you like within a function and the calling program will not be affected. The only thing the program will detect is the return value, should one exist. In this way you are protected against unpleasant side effects from calling the function.

Later you will learn ways of implementing an exchange function, the downside of which are the uncertain consequences of executing these functions.

Pointers and memory management

In the previous examples the variables have always been numerical and not strings of characters, otherwise known simply as strings. This was no accident. The treatment of strings or more generally of array variables and the associated management of memory is one of the most intractable aspects of C and C++ programming. The subject of memory is a persistent theme running through the whole book. Many other programming languages hide the problems we frankly highlight here beneath a convenient layer of abstraction. This means that you have no chance of writing highly efficient programs in these languages. The advantage of C's memory management is that it enables you to influence all these marginal conditions yourself. The disadvantage is that you need to do it in the first place.

We intend to deal with strings step by step in order to avoid leaving out anything on the way. We shall start with pointer variables and array variables, examining them both in the form of dynamically acquired memory. We shall then be not too far from our goal. Strings are basically arrays of individual characters. Don't worry if you get the feeling at some point that you have lost track of things. Once you have grasped what strings are all about the fog will lift and all the confusion will be cleared up.

3.1 The basic principle of the pointer

A pointer variable has no value of direct use to us. It merely points to another variable. A pointer to an `int` variable is of the type pointer to `int`, written `int*`. This type is used to declare variables to which `int` variables can be assigned. Assignment does not mean that the pointer variable is to assume an `int` value, but that it is to point to the `int` value. For distinguishing purposes an `&` symbol is prefixed to the assigning variable.

```
int num = 11;     // Variable number
int* numPtr;      // Pointer to number
numPtr = &num;    // numPtr now points to number
```

A counterpart to the `&` operator for assigning a variable to a pointer is the `*` operator. This operator enables the value to which the pointer is pointing to be read out.

```
cout << "numPtr points to " << *numPtr << endl;
```

This line displays

```
numPtr points to 11
```

Access to the contents of a pointer can be written as well as read, as the next line shows.

```
*numPtr = 15;
cout << "numPtr points to " << *numPtr << endl;
cout << "num has a value of " << num << endl;
```

This time

```
numPtr points to 15
num has a value of 15
```

is displayed. This tells you that it was not the pointer `numPtr` but the variable n which was altered by the assignment.

To repeat: the `&` symbol prefixed to a variable produces a pointer to the variable. The `*` symbol in front of a pointer variable produces the variable to which the pointer is pointing. In the first case we say that the variable is referenced, and in the second case that the pointer is dereferenced.

Note that the `*` symbol can mean two different things depending upon how it is used. It denotes either a variable type as in `int*`, which is a pointer variable pointing to `int`, or a variable as in `*numPtr`, to which a pointer is pointing. You get used to both meanings quite quickly, since there are in fact no circumstances in which there could be any doubt whether a type or a variable is meant.

Tip A pointer is a variable which points to a memory area occupied by another variable.

Pointer variables can be defined for any type. `char*` is a pointer to a character, and `double*` is a pointer to a floating point number. As is the case with simple variables this type categorization ensures that the compiler knows how the variable is to be interpreted.

3.2 Pointers as array variables

An interesting aspect of pointers is their use as array variables. Arrays are groups of similar variables which are merged into a new variable. At first sight it is not obvious that an array definition is equivalent to a pointer. Below is the definition of an array of three numbers.

```
int numArray[3];
```

Individual elements of the array are addressed by placing the element's index number in square brackets after the name of the array. The first index number is accessed with `numArray[0]`, the second with `numArray[1]` etc.

```
numArray[0] = 11;
numArray[1] = 22;
numArray[2] = 33;
for (int i=0; i<3; i++) {
   cout << i << " " << numArray[i] << endl;
}
```

The result is

```
0 11
1 22
2 33
```

Tip Arrays with n elements have indices 0 to n-1.

You cannot define arrays with an index other than zero. This is no great drawback, however, since you can easily add or subtract a constant value in the index if required.

All these properties suggest another way of looking at array variables already intimated at the beginning of the chapter. Array variables are pointers to the first character in the array. The square brackets indicate how many entries after the first array element the element being accessed is positioned. This is why the index starts at zero. To this extent the interpretation is a plausible one. You will see that the compiler thinks so too when you have a go at the following assignment. It does not generate an error message.

```
int* numPtr = numArray;
```

Even this type of access works.

```
cout << numPtr[2] << endl;
```

This shows you that the variable defined as a pointer can automatically be used as an array as well.

So far so good – in C++ an array just consists of a pointer to the first element. Then how does the compiler know when the array is finished? What is there to stop us accessing the element n+5 of an array with n elements? Nothing in fact! C++ is so fabulously efficient that it hasn't time to notice whether the user is reading only areas of memory to which he is actually entitled. The 3 in the square brackets of the numArray declaration applies only to the number of elements you have provided for it. It's up to you whether you then read the element numArray[6]. You should avoid doing this, of course. If you do it anyway you will usually be fed nonsense values. However, your program may terminate with the message that you have accessed prohibited areas of memory.

Whereas when you are reading elements you generally only get nonsense values, writing them is much more risky. When you assign a value to numArray[15], you are overwriting the value of some other variable which happens to be in this location in the memory. Later you wonder how come it has taken on unexpected values. The relationship to the numerical array is anything but obvious. This kind of error is very difficult to trace, and your program is likely to crash if you assign a value to an area of memory which is out of bounds to it.

3.3 Dynamically acquired memory

Occasionally you get a situation in which you want to add extra elements to an array which has already been created. This need not be due to inadequate planning on your part. Often you cannot decide how much data is required and how much has to be manipulated in the array in question until the program is actually running.

Take a program, for example, which simulates a game of roulette. It stores the stakes of the various players in an array. In the course of play more and more players may enter the game. How can you take account of these new players without choosing a huge array length in advance?

In the form used to define `numArray` the array is not expandable. In declaring the array we stipulated that `numArray` consisted of three elements. The compiler looked at the number and reserved the appropriate amount of space in the memory area available for variables. We cannot get a second bite at this because we cannot intervene once the program is running. All we can do is stop the program, write new values into the code and restart the program. But then there is a risk that we will acquire much too much memory.

What we need is a mechanism for acquiring as much memory space as the situation demands while the program is running. This can be done with the aid of dynamically acquired memory. Dynamic memory is created in a separate area of memory and is not subject to the same rigid rules as the static memory which we have been using up till now. The code for dynamically acquiring our array of three integers is as follows:

```
int* dynNumArray = new int[3];
```

As was the case previously with the static numerical array, this array is represented by a pointer variable which will point to the first character. With `new int[3]` we are acquiring new memory for three integers. The `new` operator gets us this memory and returns the pointer to its starting position. The acquisition of dynamic memory is also called allocating dynamic memory.

Tip Dynamic memory is acquired using `new`.

A word to the C programmers among you who were expecting the keyword `malloc` at this point instead of `new`. The two keywords have the same function, but only `new` is consistent with C++ memory management and is therefore preferred.

The dynamically created numerical array is used in exactly the same way as the statically created array. We can assign values to the array elements and read them out again.

```
dynNumArray[1] = 11;
cout << dynNumArray[1] << endl;
```

The rule here as before is that it is up to you to make sure that the array limits are not exceeded.

As soon as the numerical array is no longer required we have to dispense with it. This is the price we pay for the advantages of the dynamic memory. Since we did not acquire the memory until the program was run, the compiler is in no position to free it again. So we do it ourselves with the aid of the `delete` operator.

```
delete[] dynNumArray;
```

> **Tip** Dynamically acquired memory is freed again using `delete`.

Now we have the tools at our disposal to make an array with five elements out of an array with two elements. The whole thing is a bit more tricky than you might at first imagine, but is nevertheless convincing.

We cannot simply stick three extra elements on an array of two elements. We have to rely on the fact that all the elements in the new array are located in a single contiguous block of memory. The only safe procedure for obtaining five successive memory locations is to allocate them as a whole. The old array of two elements can then be freed, but not before we have copied its contents to the beginning of the new array.

The following code implements this operation. We use here a temporary variable `dynNumArrayTmp` which points to the new array as long as the contents of the old array are being copied into it.

```
// Acquire and use array with two elements
int* dynNumArray = new int[2];
...
// Acquire array with 5 elements as required
int* dynNumArrayTmp = new int[5];
// Copy contents into it
dynNumArrayTmp[0] = dynNumArray[0];
dynNumArrayTmp[1] = dynNumArray[1];
// Free old array
delete[] dynNumArray;
// Assign temporary pointer to old pointer
dynNumArray = dynNumArrayTmp;
// Use dynNumArray with 5 elements
...
// Free large array again at the end
delete[] dynNumArray;
```

Programming this procedure may be a bit longwinded, but you can rest assured that it is extremely efficient. In other programming languages this type of code is generated automatically and as a result is encumbered with a lot of unnecessary baggage.

Dynamically acquired arrays differ from static arrays in another detail. A variable can be used for the length of a dynamic array instead of a fixed number. This in itself does full justice to its name, since it is the only way of allocating the exact amount of memory required at run time. To illustrate this we shall attempt to write some lines which acquire n numbers both statically and dynamically. Since the number n is a variable, the compiler cannot compile the request for static memory.

```
int n = 12;
int* dynNumArray = new int[n];    // OK
int numArray[n];                  // Not compilable!
```

This difference can again be explained by the fact that static memory is provided by the compiler and in fixed amounts, whereas dynamic memory is not created until the program is run.

We have always been very conscientious about freeing the memory again once it has been acquired. This might seem a bit petty. We don't indulge ourselves with 128 MB or more of main memory for nothing. How much more you can judge for yourself via the following endless loop. It causes your program to crash as soon as the memory reserved for it has been exhausted. The loop condition we use is simply the keyword `true` .

```
for (int i=1; true; i++) {
  char* oneMegabyte = new char[1024*1024];
  cout << i << " MB are acquired." << endl;
}
```

 If your total is unexpectedly high this will be because besides the physical main memory part of your hard disc is used as virtual main memory. A

```
delete[] oneMegabyte;
```

inserted before the end of the loop will cause the program to run continuously.

> **Warning** If you forget to free dynamic memory your program may crash due to lack of memory.

We have now almost reached our goal, the string. At this point, for the sake of completeness, we shall briefly show you how simple variables can be dynamically allocated as well as arrays. This is not a particularly useful operation at the moment, but its importance will become clearer as soon as we begin to deal with objects. Dynamically created simple variables are used in exactly the same way as dynamically created array variables except that the square brackets are discarded in both `new` and `delete`. You will be familiar with the assignment of values via the * operator from the example of pointers which point to simple static variables.

```
double* dynFloatNum = new double;
*dynFloatNum = 1.234;
delete dynFloatNum;
```

The first two lines can be combined by using the shorthand form

```
double* dynFloatNum = new double (1.234);
```

3.4 Strings

A string is a special case of an array variable. A string is an array of characters instead of the numbers we have seen in previous examples. As a rule you will not know in advance how many characters are needed, or you will not want to specify a particular number. You therefore have to acquire the necessary memory dynamically at run time.

```
char* word = new char[10];
```

This creates an array of ten characters. word[n] is of the type char.

Tip Strings are declared as char*.

String arrays basically function just like numerical arrays. However, there are a number of auxiliary functions which simplify the use of character arrays as strings. If you make these available in your program with

```
#include <string.h>
```

you can fill the whole array with values using

```
strcpy (word, "Caribbean");
```

instead of laboriously entering each character individually as

```
word[0] = 'C';
word[1] = 'a';
...
```

The text in quotation marks "Caribbean" is a practical example of an array of characters with fixed content. You can always use text in quotation marks synonymously with char* variables provided that you don't try to assign them a value. It's now clear what the function of strcpy is – it simply copies all the elements from one character array into another character array. But strcpy does even more than just copy the nine characters of the word Caribbean. It adds a zero byte as the tenth character. The job of the zero byte is to mark the end of the string. The word `"Caribbean"` implicitly contains the zero byte too. All functions and instructions involved in string processing keep to this convention, including `cout`.

```
cout << "The content of word is " << word << "." << endl;
```

outputs

```
The content of word is Caribbean.
```

Without the zero byte `cout` would not recognize where `word` ends.

> **Tip** Strings end in a zero byte.

You must be careful not to confuse the zero byte with the figure 0. Zero byte refers to the character with an ASCII value of 0, which is written in program code as '\0'.

You now know the rules for processing strings. You have also learned the more general rules for the management of dynamic memory. With the help of a few examples we shall now illustrate some of the quirks of the string concept. How about the string for the name Jackie, for instance?

```
char* name = new char[6];
strcpy (name, "Jackie");
```

This is a case of surreptitious access to a memory location which has not been reserved for your program. But you have acquired six characters and copied the six characters in "Jackie" – so what's the problem? The catch lies with the lack of a zero byte at the end of Jackie, it has to be there too. The correct procedure would have been to acquire seven characters. The penalty for imprecision is false values in other variables or crashed programs, the latter being the lesser evil, they are easier to trace.

The consequences of forgetting the final zero byte are demonstrated by the following piece of code.

```
char* wo = new char[3];
wo[0] = 'w';
wo[1] = 'o ';
cout << wo << endl;
```

The output of cout will end in the next zero byte which happens to be in the memory. It might be wo§rz/5??.,dfg, or it might be something completely different beginning with wo.

On the other hand, too many zero bytes can also produce unexpected results.

```
char* myName = new char [strlen ("Matthew") +1];
strcpy (myName, "Matthew");
myName[3] = '\0';
cout << myName << endl;
```

The output in this case is Mat, not Matthew. Incidentally, you have just seen in action the function strlen which defines the length of a string and saves you a lot of arduous counting. You must make sure, however, that strlen does not include the zero byte in its count.

3.5 Other properties of pointers

3.5.1   Flat and deep copies

There is a famous example of string copying which at first sight is a bit confusing. Initially the variables source and target are defined. source points to a string, target does not, see Figure 3.1.

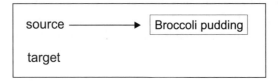

Figure 3.1 *Starting point*

```
char* source = new char [strlen ("Broccoli pudding") +1];
strcpy (source, "Broccoli pudding");
char* target;
```

The task is to make a copy of `source` in `target`. Our first attempt is as brief as it is plausible, but it is not totally successful.

```
target = source;
```

Following this assignment the contents of both pointers are as expected and can be displayed using `cout`.

```
cout << source << endl;
cout << target << endl;
```

The output is

```
Broccoli pudding
Broccoli pudding
```

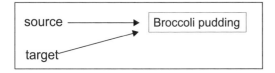

Figure 3.2 *A flat copy*

But altering the text of `source` affects the text referenced by `target`.

```
source[8] = '\0';
cout << source << endl;
cout << target << endl;
```

The output is now

```
Broccoli
Broccoli
```

This is not what one expects from a self-respecting copy operation, i.e. that it should be independent of the original. In fact what has happened is that the `target` pointer has been pointed at the same contents to which the `source` pointer is pointing, see Figure 3.2.

What we should have done is define new memory equivalent to the length of the text for the `target` pointer and then copy the area of memory pointed to by the `source` pointer into this new memory. Our second much more successful attempt then looks like this:

```
target = new char [strlen (source) +1];
strcpy (target, source);
```

For both variables `cout` displays identical outputs as before. But if we again alter the text pointed to by `source`, the contents of `target` remain unchanged:

```
Broccoli
Broccoli pudding
```

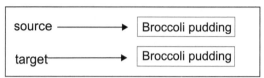

Figure 3.3 *A deep copy*

Situations such as this are not infrequent when you are dealing with strings. The example in which only the contents of the pointer were copied is called a flat copy. The second example is known as a deep copy, since the area of memory following the source pointer was also copied, see Figure 3.3. Both procedures are legitimate ones. The second meets all the requirements of a genuine copy. The first is useful only if you can be certain that the original has not been changed. Since it involves fewer copy operations it is much more efficient.

3.5.2   Non-directional pointers

Sometimes one finds oneself in the awkward position of defining a pointer variable without having an area of memory to which it could point. It would be nice in this situation to be able to assign a well-defined value to the pointer. This value should signify that the pointer has indeed been defined but that it does not yet point anywhere. In C++ this well-defined non-directional pointer value is called `NULL`. We can write, for example:

```
char* word = NULL;
```

If you want to output the word later, you can first ask whether it has been defined.

```
if (word == NULL) {
  cout << "word is unoccupied. " << endl;
}
else {
  cout << "the contents of word are " << word << endl;
}
```

Tip By using `NULL` a pointer can be made deliberately non-directional.

The NULL pointer has a special significance in relation to the `delete` operator for freeing memory.

```
char* word = NULL;
delete word;
```

Had you instead left `word` alone, your program would very probably have crashed, since a pointer which has not been initialized can have any value whatsoever. `delete` would then have tried to free an area of memory which was never acquired with `new`.

3.5.3   Type security

The compiler is quite meticulous about distinguishing between types of pointer. This is particularly important when pointers are assigned to each other. Whereas the compiler's usual response to an assignment between different simple types of variable is just a warning, it draws a line in this case as the following example shows:

```
char charact = 'A';
char* charactPtr = &charact;
int num = 66;
int* numPtr = &num;
charactPtr = numPtr;          // Will not compile!
```

It's far too easy for unseen errors to creep in in this manner. If on the other hand you are really sure that the assignment is a sensible one you can use cast, though you must handle such an expression with extreme care.

```
charactPtr = (char*) numPtr;  // Will compile
```

When you add the lines

```
cout << *numPtr << endl;
cout << *charactPtr << endl;
```

you will not get the same value 66 twice as you might suppose, but

```
66
B
```

because of the type difference the same symbol is interpreted first as a number and then as a character. Sixty-six is the ASCII value for 'B'.

3.6 The parameters of a program

With all the background knowledge we have gained we can now try out pointers in a practical environment. C++ views an array of pointers as parameters for the main program `main`. It is not only methods which use parameters. The behavior of whole programs can be influenced by call parameters. As a rule technical parameters are passed to a program for all its future life. For example you can specify buffer sizes or stipulate whether the program once started is to behave as a client or a server. The user can even run a command line oriented program. Many DOS or UNIX shell commands have access to a simple call interface, via which the user can specify files for processing or execution parameters. A command such as `cd` for changing the directory works as follows:

```
cd c:\data
```

The parameters passed can be of completely different types, and so the C++ main program returns them as strings. One variant of the function `main` which you can use is shown below.

```
int main (int argc, char* argv[])
```

The expression `argc` contains the number n of parameters in question. `argv` is an array of n+1 strings. The first string in the parameter array `argv[0]` holds the name of the program called and the following arrays contain the parameters.

The integer return value is also significant. It indicates whether the program has been error-free. At least that is the significance which other programs attach to your program's return value and which you should give it. In the C canon a return value of zero denotes a successfully executed function or a successfully executed program. All other return values are interpreted as error codes.

The following main program is typical in the way it functions. It expects at least one parameter, otherwise it terminates with an error code of 1. A 1 is often used as an error code if there is no need to distinguish individual cases of error. If a program is called with the parameter –h it displays a short description of the call syntax. We compare the parameter with the string `"-h"` with the aid of the function `strcmp`. It is part of the standard library of C and C++, similar to the `strcpy` function which copies memory contents. `strcmp` compares the areas of memory defined by the two pointer parameters up to the first zero byte and returns a zero if they are identical. If you call the program with the parameters in question you will obtain the following output:

```
Call: prog <file name>
```

You will see from the accompanying code that the program name `prog` is not hard-wired and is not defined from the parameter `argv[0]` until the program is running. This makes sense since you can give the program any name you like.

If at least one parameter has been passed and the first one is not the same as -h, the program interprets it as the expected file name. It is passed on to the function `mainfunction` which processes it appropriately. All other parameters are ignored.

The main function makes it clear via its return value whether it has been able to complete its task successfully. If it returns any error number other than zero the program as a whole returns an error code of 1. Otherwise success is signaled by a return value of zero. The statement `exit` does for the program as a whole what `return` does for a function – it terminates it.

```cpp
#include <string.h>
int main_function (char* a) { ... }
int main (int argc, char* argv[]) {
  if (argc == 1) {
    exit (1);
  }
  else {
    if (strcmp(argv[1],"-h") == 0) {
      cout << "Call: " << argv[0]
           << " <file name>" << endl;
      exit (0);
    }
    if (main_function (argv[1]) == 0) {
      exit (0);
    } else {
      exit (1);
    }
  }
}
```

Objects

You have been introduced to functions as one means of giving large programs a well-structured framework. Functions are quite widely applicable, but they have the disadvantage that it is you who has to ensure that they are fed the correct data.

The bigger the program, the more parameters you have to supply for your functions in order to feed the sub-functions called, and their sub-functions in turn, with the correct values. Or you can avoid the issue by having recourse to global variables. These are variables which are defined outside the scope of any block and are therefore accessible in all parts of the program. You then have to hope that your functions are so clearly coded that they do not get in each other's way when accessing these data.

Both procedures are merely ways of circumventing the fact that data and the functions used to manipulate them form a logical whole. This should be reflected in the structure of your program too! The corresponding C++ construct is called an object.

Tip An object consists of data and associated functions.

Besides linking data and functions, object-oriented programming also satisfies the human need for transparency. It offers the possibility of using objects from the real world as simple variables in a program. In C++ by analogy with the elementary type `int` you can, for example, define your own type `motorcycle`. This type can contain all kinds of complex properties and is as simple to use as a numerical type. Instead of

```
int val = 92;
cout << val << endl;
```

C++ allows you to define a variable of the type `motorcycle` and manipulate it.

```
motorcycle matthewsDucati (92);   // Ducati at 92 h.p.
matthewsDucati.accelerate ();
```

Whether the type `motorcycle` stands for a simulator or merely an entry in a vehicle data bank depends purely and simply on how `motorcycle` is defined. This as we have said is up to you. Object-oriented programming will be a great help to you in structuring your programs, but you are not absolved from the responsibility of programming the way they actually function.

However this less than perfect transparency is one of the merits of objects. You can change the way an object is implemented without changing the way it is used. The object simply conceals the underlying code and presents you with a concise interface to its properties. You often begin with a simple implementation. You can then use the object in your programs straight away and provide the more developed implementation code later.

A word or two about the name. It has become established practice to call object types classes. Thus `matthewsDucati` is an object of the class `motorcycle`. This makes clearer the contrast with elementary types such as `int`. For the same reason the functions of a class are called methods. `accelerate` is a method of the class `motorcycle`. We shall also stick to this convention.

In the specialist literature you will often come across the term "instance" when a member of a class, i.e. an object, is meant. In fact it is so widely used that we too shall refer to instantiation in this book when an object is created.

With the topic of objects we leave classical C country and enter completely the world of C++.

Citing the example of the Ducati so soon is perhaps aiming a bit high, but we can always start with a simple implementation of it. The definition of a motorcycle class might look like this:

```
class Motorcycle {
private:
  int aHP;
};
```

The first question to ask when creating this class is what data does it use? The data variables of a class are also called attributes. In order to distinguish a class's attributes from other variables we shall add a lower case a in front of its name. Although this or a similar identification symbol is widely used, it is not prescribed as a C++ term anywhere in the language definition. The Motorcycle class contains the attribute aHP. It is declared in the same way as other variables. In order to ensure that it will not be manipulated in undesirable ways by mischievous users it has the expression private attached to it. aHP cannot be modified by elements in the program which do not belong to the class.

> **Tip** The data variables of an object are called attributes, its functions are called methods.

Next a constructor is required. A constructor is a method of defining how an object of the class in question is initialized. In order to highlight the special role of the constructor it is given the same name as the class itself. This is part of the C++ language definition. Moreover the constructor never has a return value. To avoid your having to precede it with a void it is omitted altogether.

The next thing to do is to give the constructor of Motorcycle a parameter hp which is assigned to the attribute aHP. Every user of this class will need the constructor whenever he wants to initialize an object, and so it is given the attachment public. So far then the class Motorcycle looks like this:

```
class Motorcycle {
public:
  Motorcycle (int hp) {
    aHP = hp;
  }
private:
  int aHP;
};
```

Tip A constructor is a method for creating an object.

At the moment `Motorcycle` consists only of a variable and a method of initialization, and the class does nothing. This can be changed by the addition of a method for acceleration. The code is simple.

```
class Motorcycle {
public:
  Motorcycle (int hp) {
    aHP = hp;
  }
  void accelerate () {
    cout << "The machine accelerates at "
         << aHP << " h.p." << endl;
  }
private:
  int aHP;
};
```

Note that the method `accelerate` has access to the attribute even though it was not passed as a parameter.

Now the `Motorcycle` class can be used from the main program like an elementary data type. An executable program using `Motorcycle` might look like this:

```
#include <iostream.h>
class Motorcycle {
  ...  // See above
};
main () {
  // Create two objects of the type Motorcycle
  Motorcycle matthewsDucati (92);
  Motorcycle robertsXT (35);
  // Accelerate both machines
  matthewsDucati.accelerate ();
  robertsXT.accelerate ();
}
```

The output of this program is

```
The machine accelerates at 92 h.p.
The machine accelerates at 35 h.p.
```

Even if you recognize intuitively how the four lines in the main program work, it is important that you are clear about their exact meaning.

```
Motorcycle matthewsDucati (92);
```

creates an object named `matthewsDucati` of the class `Motorcycle`. Also this line implicitly calls the constructor of `Motorcycle`. In this way the attribute receives the value passed of 92.

The line

```
matthewsDucati.accelerate ();
```

calls the method `accelerate` of the object `matthewsDucati` just created. One of its effects is to output the value of 92 previously defined. Method calls are generally in the form of

```
<object>.<method> ();
```

or

```
<return value> = <object>.<method> (<list of parameters>);
```

if there are parameters present.

Although all the programming you have been shown hitherto has been purely functional, you should pause for a moment and savor one of the peculiarities of the small main program. First the object `matthewsDucati` was created, and then the object `robertsXT`. Both fit into our scheme of things, since they are merely unusual forms of function call.

What is odd, however, is the fact that calling the method `accelerate` can access a variable which had been miraculously deposited in the preceding constructor call, namely `aHP`. This is what object-oriented programming does for you. Objects are places for depositing the data used by their methods. You could have achieved a similar effect up till now only by using global variables. Otherwise all that remained of a pure function call was the return value.

4.2 Destructors

Have a look at the class `Text` below which makes strings easier to use. It has a pointer as an attribute named `aTextPtr`. Its constructor also gets a pointer passed to it as a parameter. It makes a deep copy of this pointer which it assigns to the pointer attribute. `Text` also contains a method for displaying the string.

```
class Text {
public:
  Text (char* textPtr) {
    aTextPtr = new char [strlen(textPtr) +1];
    strcpy (aTextPtr, textPtr);
  }
  void output () {
    cout << aTextPtr << endl;
  }
private:
  char* aTextPtr;
};
```

Text can be used like this:

```
Text alphabet ("ABC...XYZ");
alphabet.output ();
```

But what happens to the area of memory which was acquired in the constructor?
Who frees it when the object is no longer needed? At the moment nobody. You
can try executing a test program using an endless loop. The program still crashes
very quickly.

```
while (true) {
  Text alphabet ("ABC...XYZ");
}
```

In order to prevent this happening C++ provides another special method apart
from the constructor, i.e. a destructor. The task of the destructor is to deal with
any clearing up operations which are needed when an object ceases to exist. In
the majority of cases this means freeing up memory previously acquired by the
object. The destructor bears the name of the class preceded by a tilde (~). Destructors have no parameters.

```
class Text {
public:
  Text (char* textPtr) {
    aTextPtr = new char [strlen(textPtr) +1];
    strcpy (aTextPtr, textPtr);
  }
  ~Text () {
    delete[] aTextPtr;
  }
  void output () {
    cout << aTextPtr << endl;
  }
```

```
private:
  char* aTextPtr;
};
```

Whereas a call to a constructor is halfway recognizable, calls to destructors are virtually undetectable. The destructor is automatically called when the associated object is destroyed, i.e. when the block in which it is embedded is vacated. Since `Text` now has a destructor, the endless loop really runs endlessly.

```
while (true) {
  Text alphabet ("ABC...XYZ");
}  // Implicit call to destructor
```

In this context it is essential that we distinguish between two facts. Like any other variable the object `alphabet` is destroyed when it ceases to be valid. This occurs irrespective of whether `Text` has a destructor or not. In the example the sole function of the destructor is to free the acquired memory to which the attribute `aTextPtr` is pointing.

All will be well if you stick to the basic rule which we have observed when implementing the `Text` class.

> **Tip** Every class with a pointer attribute should define a destructor in which the referenced memory is freed.

As the book progresses `Text` will gradually be expanded into a tool which will finally be all you could wish for. The final version is printed in the Appendix to avoid having to show the complete code each time we add to it.

4.3 Encapsulation

The fact that objects combine data and functions into a whole seems reasonable enough. The fact that life is made unnecessarily difficult in that the object's data is protected from use by other classes by attaching the keyword `private` may seem a bit excessive. But this is not the case at all.

An object's attributes are not concealed out of secretiveness but in order to safeguard their consistency. A class which contains percentages for an election result must ensure that one hundred percent of each party's share of the votes are added up. You can make sure of this only by representing the various percentages by private variables and allowing them to be manipulated only via publicly accessible methods. The methods must be written in such a way that after they have been called there is always a total of one hundred percent remaining. The user of a class, who is not infrequently the writer of the program, cannot be expected to keep an eye on these relationships.

Or consider the significance of the `private` keyword attached to the pointer attribute in the `Text` class. You know how dangerous it is if pointers point to the wrong location. The `output` method itself yields weird values if you are careless about defining the pointer `aTextPtr` somewhere in your code. Your program is at risk of coming to a sudden end if the destructor attempts with the aid of `delete` to free an area of memory which has not previously been acquired via `new`. Therefore direct access to the pointer attribute must definitely be avoided.

In the following somewhat provocative example you will see an attempt to change the text pointer directly. Fortunately the compiler stops this assignment from occurring and the program from crashing at the final curly brackets.

```
#include <iostream.h>
class Text {
   ...
};
main () {
   {
     Text myText("Himalayas");
     myText.output ();
     myText.aTextPtr = 13; // Cannot compile!
   }  // Implicit call to destructor
   ...
}
```

You should declare the attribute of a class as `private` in order to safeguard its consistency.

The separation of the public and non-public characteristics of a class can be taken even further. We can also pass methods to the part of the class declared as `private` so that it does its job as an internal auxiliary function. The output method could for example be reserved for debugging purposes in a more complex implementation of the text class. If a method is declared in the `private` section of a class definition, it can be called only from other methods of the same class, and not from other classes.

Besides a number of other public methods the class `FormattedText`, which is briefly introduced below, has a method for changing its line length attribute. This automatically results in a change in the number of lines since the number of characters in a text remains constant. Errors may well have occurred during the programming of this section, and so the developer has decided to log each change in the line length. To do this he uses the private method `attribute-Output`.

```
class FormattedText {
public:
  // A number of methods
  ...
  setLineLength (int length) {
    // Change line length, adjust number of lines
    ...
    attributeOutput ();   // For debugging only
  }
private:
  attributeOutput () {
    cout << "Line length" << aLineLength << endl;
    cout << "Number of lines" << aNumberLines << endl;
  }
  int aLineLength;
  int aNumberLines;
};
```

Since the method `attributeOutput` cannot be called from outside this class, it is removed by the developer when the test phase is finished. The `private` declaration ensures that no other program uses this method and that consequently no other program is disturbed by its removal.

To make your life a little easier C++ treats all attributes and methods as `private` unless you explicitly declare them as `public`. Specially creating public attributes should be a conscious decision.

4.4 Separation of interface and implementation

The notion of encapsulation of objects embodies another technique which is not restricted to object-oriented languages. We refer to the partitioning of interface and implementation details in separate files. So what is an implementation detail, and what is an interface?

The methods of the `Text` class are certainly part of an interface since they define the way the class is used. Every user must know about a program's methods and their parameters if he wishes to employ them. On the other hand he will have little interest in how the constructor and the `output` method are implemented. Texts may be filed in a tree structure or they may be in a fixed-length field, the user has no influence over these matters.

The two aspects need to be separated if, for example, the implementation of a class is a valuable industrial secret, but the class is nevertheless to be sold to customers. For this purpose we can make the plain interface description of the class available to the user in a separate file, whereas the class's implementation is kept hidden in the .cpp file. This means dividing up the `Text` class into the files `text.h` and `text.cpp`, where the ending .h denotes header. We shall employ here the file-ending `.cpp` to represent all the common variants such as `.cc` and `.cxx` which different compilers use to identify the implementation file. In its special development environment the header file can also have a short ending other than `.h`.

The header file contains all the information there is about how the class is linked together as a whole. Only the method code is omitted, and we pay for this with an extra semicolon after the function header. Truncated methods such as these are also called method declarations. They merely give advance notice of the actual implementation which follows later.

file `text.h`:

```
class Text {
public:
  // Constructor
  Text (char* textPtr);
  // Destructor
  ~Text ();
  // Output method
  void output ();
private:
  char* aTextPtr;
};
```

It subsequently passes into the `.cpp` file. In this case we talk about a method definition. Since all methods are listed independently of each other in the `.cpp` file, the method name is preceded by the class name followed by `::`. This is the only way the compiler has of distinguishing methods from normal functions.

file `text.cpp`:

```
// Constructor
Text::Text (char* textPtr) {
  textPtr = new char[strlen(textPtr)+1];
  strcpy (aTextPtr, textPtr);
}
// Destructor
Text::~Text () {
  delete[] aTextPtr;
}
// Output method
void Text::output () {
```

```
  cout << aTextPtr << endl;
}
```

We shall frequently come across the notation :: when we have to state the class to which a variable or a method belongs. We say that a class's methods and attributes form a common namespace. The double colon is also called a scope resolution operator or button operator.

The .cpp file can now be sent to the customer in compiled form. He will just see the .h file in plain text. This is all the information he needs in order to use the class in his own code. He can incorporate the Text class in his programs with an include statement. You will be familiar with this operation from the file iostream.h which we always incorporate when we wish to output data via cout. Self-written header files in contrast to system headers have to have the ending .h in the include statement. Quotation marks are used instead of angle brackets.

A program using our text class in two-part form might look like this:

```
#include "text.h"
main () {
  Text text ("Include test");
  text.output ();
}
```

The split variants of text have the additional advantage for our fictitious customer that it is easier for him to gain an overview of the way the class functions. The header file – hopefully provided with meaningful comments – is much easier to read than the complete code of the class.

We explain in Part II Chapter 14 how you compile a program divided among several files. In that chapter you will also find a discussion of the creation and use of class libraries.

In this book advantage is always taken of a separate class definition whenever it is the structure of a class alone, which is important to the explanation. The scope resolution notation for method implementations is useful if a single method only is being described, since you can see at once to what class it belongs.

In this and the foregoing chapter two different approaches to the visibility of implementation details have been considered. In one a programmer secures the independence of parts of a program via private attributes and methods by hiding the internal details of his classes from other classes. This is visibility in terms of the outside classes ability to call. The other approach enables the programmer to keep the human-readable elements of his class implementation to himself and to pass on to other programmers the class structure as an interface. This is visibility in terms of readability by outside programmers.

Both forms of visibility or invisibility can be combined at will. The code of public methods can be held in a `.cpp` file just as the code of `private` methods can be placed directly in the class definition.

4.5 Dynamically created objects

Objects as well as variables can be created dynamically. This is the point where the detailed preliminary work we did on pointers pays off. To a large extent we can adopt the familiar syntax when we wish to create dynamic objects. Below a pointer to a `text` object is declared and provided with a newly instantiated text.

```
Text* textPtr = new Text ("Weekend");
```

The freeing of an object referenced by a pointer occurs in the same manner and with the same necessity as it did in the case of pointers to simple variables. Since destructors are always executed when the associated object is destroyed, one is called here by the addition of `delete`.

```
delete textPtr;  // Call destructor and free object
```

The methods of dynamically allocated objects are accessed in a different way. This is obvious, since simple variables have no methods. We are already familiar, however, with the * operator for accessing a variable referenced by a pointer. We can use that here too. With

```
(*textPtr).output ();
```

we can call the text class's output method. More common, however, is a shorthand form which means the same thing.

```
textPtr->output ();
```

The attributes of a dynamically created object are accessed in the same way as methods. As a rule, of course, we have declared attributes as `private` and so they were not accessible from outside. For demonstration purposes only we are going to break the rules of encapsulation and use the class `NotPrivate` to access a public attribute.

```
class NotPrivate {
public:
  int aNum;
};
```

In this way we can use a pointer to access the attribute of `NotPrivate`.

```
// Allocate object dynamically
NotPrivate* npPtr = new NotPrivate;
// Access attribute, concise notation
npPtr->aNum = 8;
cout << npPtr->aNum<< endl;
// Access attribute, fuller notation
(*npPtr).aNum = 9;
cout << (*npPtr).aNum << endl;
// Don't forget to free memory
delete npPtr;
```

The casual-sounding comment "Don't forget to free memory" highlights once more the problems of memory management, the seriousness of which cannot be overemphasized in relation to the manipulation of pointers. A program which does not free redundant dynamic memory consumes more and more memory as time passes. This is fine, until the point when all the memory is used up. The program, or else one of the simultaneously running programs, then terminates. This is tantamount to pre-programming functional errors.

For this reason you should acquire dynamic memory only when you really need it and make sure to free it again when it has been used. If you use simple variables instead of pointers the compiler will do the freeing for you. The example program which demonstrated the use of attributes can easily be implemented without pointers. As you know, a simple object's destructor is called when it ceases to be visible.

Since simple variables free memory by themselves when they vacate their associated block, they are also called automatic variables. There are few reasons to prefer dynamic variables to automatic variables. The main one is that you do not find out until run time how many instances of a type you actually need in an array.

You have already come across this principle in the variable-length texts implemented as `char*`. Or in the roulette game where we were not sure in advance how many players would be taking part. For this latter example we could implement a class `Bet` comprising a stake, the associated array and the person placing the bet. We need not worry too much about these classes, but one thing they must possess, and that is a parameterless constructor.

```
class Bet{
public:
  // Parameterless constructor
  Bet () {...}
  ...
};
```

As soon as you know how many bets are placed you can allocate an array of bets using `new` and free it again later using `delete[]`.

```
n = ...;
Bet* betList = new Bet[n];
// Use betList
if (n>0) {
  betList [0].output ();
}
// Free betList again
delete[] betList;
```

The class `Bet` plays the same role here as the elementary types `char` or `int` in previous examples. Calling `new` in the case of classes not only acquires memory for the n `Bet` objects but also summons their parameterless constructors. Correspondingly `delete[]` calls the destructors of all `Bet` objects of the array before it destroys them.

4.6 Inheritance

When you are writing a program you often have the suspicion that you have already programmed something similar. The old code could be reused but for this or that small difference between the old and the new code. Too often you take the coward's way out and write the program all over again. Or you simply take a copy of the tried and tested program and use it as a basis for the new one. And so, as time passes, like parts of programs are married with like parts of other programs without any benefit being gained from all this common material.

The object-oriented programming wizards have a solution for this too. The buzzword is inheritance. This construct makes it possible to define a new class with the aid of an existing one and to expand it into a set of new programming functions. The inheritance concept also allows the properties of the original class to be changed.

Using this principle we are going to write a class for date arrays. We shall make use of another class which we might have created before for another purpose, a class for pairs of numbers. It will have two integer attributes, aNum1 and aNum2, which can be defined from within a constructor. A second constructor is parameterless and sets the attributes to neutral values only. The class `Pair` has a method which outputs the two attributes separated by a space. Furthermore it has two `set` methods for setting the attributes and two `get` methods for interrogating them. Methods such as these for accessing attributes are widespread, but their name is not prescribed in the language definition.

```
class Pair {
public:
  Pair (int num1, int num2) {
    aNum1 = num1;
    aNum2 = num2;
  }
  Pair () {
    aNum1 = 0;
    aNum2 = 0;
  }
  void output () {
    cout << aNum1 << " " << aNum2 << endl;
  }
  setNum1 (int num) {
    aNum1 = num;
  }
  setNum2 (int num) {
    aNum2 = num;
  }
private:
  int aNum1;
  int aNum2;
};
```

A user can use this class in the following manner:

```
Pair numPair (12, 34);
numPair.output ();
numPair.setNum2 (21);
numPair.output ();
```

These lines display

```
12 34
12 21
```

We want the date class to inherit two of its integer attributes, the day and the month, from the `Pair` class. The attribute for the year is added later. We must ensure that the class `Pair` is known in the part of the program in which the class `Date` is defined. We deal with this by locating the definition of `pair` in the same file preceding the definition of `Date`. It is actually more elegant to split the class `Pair` into two separate files as we did for the class `Text`. Then the header file `pair.h` can be made available for the definition of `Date` with the aid of the include statement.

```
#include "pair.h"
class Date : public Pair {
private:
  int aYear;   // The year
};
```

The colon in the class definition tells us that Date is derived from Pair, i.e. inherits from Pair. This happens publicly (public) so that the class Date can also access the attributes of Pair.

Next a constructor is needed which allows a definition such as

```
Date petersBirthday (15,3,72);
```

And of course we still have no suitable output function.

```
#include "pair.h"
class Date : public Pair {
public:
  Date (int day, int month, int year) {
    // Set attributes of Pair
    setNum1 (day);
    setNum2 (month);
    // Set new attribute
    aYear = year;
  }
  void output () {
    cout << getNum1() << "." << getNum2() << ".";
        << aYear << endl;
  }
private:
  int aYear;   // The year
};
```

You can see that the methods of Pair can be used inside the newly defined class Date without an object name being needed. Methods of the class such as functions can be called within a class definition. This also applies to methods of the class from which they have been derived. However, the class Date cannot access the private attributes of Pair, they are protected from it too.

Tip The concept of inheritance enables us to define a new class with the help of an existing class. The new class can use and expand the attributes and methods of the original class.

The constructor is readily identified as an additional piece of functional code, although it has a different name from the constructor of `Pair`. But the method `output` looks like it could be mixed up with the original of the same name in the original class. Fortunately this does not happen. If you define a method in a derived class which has a corresponding definition in the parent class the former is simply overridden. The following test case proves that overriding does in fact work.

```
Date jillsBirthday (1,1,1976);   // The constructor
jillsBirthday.output ();         // displays 1.1.1976
```

Overriding, incidentally, is the special term used to describe the redefinition of a method of the same name in a derived class. The class from which another class has been derived by inheritance is called a base class or parent class. `Pair` is a base class of `Date`. `Date` in turn is called a derived or child class of `Pair`.

You do not necessarily have to implement the methods of the base class all over again in a derived class as we did in the case of `output`. If you are happy with your version of the base class you can leave it as it is. Nevertheless you can see how useful it is from the fact that a method such as `getNum1`, which is defined only in `Pair`, can be called without any difficulty for a `Date` object.

```
cout << jillsBirthday.getNum1 () << endl;
```

On the other hand you have a chance to define methods in the derived class which have no equivalents in the base class. The constructor of `Date` is an example of this, but we can also attach a quite normal method to `Date` which would make no sense in the base class.

```
class Date : public Pair {
public:
  int getYear () {
    return aYear;
  }
  ...   // The rest as before
}
```

This method can be called for each `Date` object, but not for a `Pair` object.

```
cout << jillsBirthday.getYear () << endl;
```

Public inheritance has a further feature, namely a `Date` object can be regarded in many respects like a `Pair` object, though a special one. For example, a pointer to a `Date` object is at the same time a pointer to a `Pair` object. For this no type conversion is needed.

```
Date* datePtr = new Date (22,2,2222);
Pair* pairPtr = datePtr;   // Compile without warning
```

The obverse does not apply, however. This is plausible, since a `Pair` object is endowed with many fewer attributes and methods than a `Date` object.

```
Pair* pairPtr = new Pair (3,3);
Date* datePtr = pairPtr;  // Does not compile!
```

In the same manner as we derived the class `Date` from the class `Pair` we can define derivation hierarchies of any length. Ideally the inheritance relationship would be formed less arbitrarily than it is here. In fact it is worthwhile including in your planning whole groups of classes which are to figure together in an inheritance relationship. Then it makes perfect sense to derive several child classes from the same parent class. This generally results in a tree-type structure. The relationship between `Pair` and `Date` is typical of more complex derivation trees in that the base class is more abstract in nature than a class which has been derived from it.

A possible derivation tree for a number of classes representing vehicles of various types is shown in Figure 4.1.

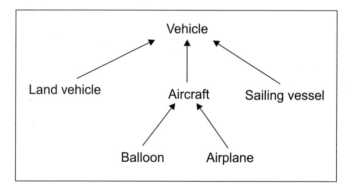

Figure 4.1 *Derivation hierarchy for vehicle classes*

The class `Land vehicle` inherits the properties of `Vehicle`, and the class `Balloon` inherits those of `Aircraft` including the properties of `Vehicle`. In a class diagram such as this we usually put the base class at the top. The derived classes are arranged below and connected by arrows to the associated base class. The arrow points from the derived class to the base class.

We can use this kind of diagram to find out which classes have properties in common and which classes behave differently when we modify a base class.

The greater whole 5

The aim of the first part of the book was to give you an insight into C++ programming as rapidly as possible. You were introduced to the elementary statements for loops and conditional statements, as well as simple variable types. You practiced handling pointers, you defined functions and finally you implemented classes.

With these language tools in your toolbox you can knock together respectable programs which carry out the most varied tasks. Still missing from a comprehensive overview, however, is a description of the objectives which C++ sets itself. Where do its strengths lie in comparison with other programming languages? What properties can we expect to find? Which ones will we look for in vain? Absorb the import of these objectives and you are more likely to appreciate the features of the language which we consider to be of particular significance in the main part of the book. And you will be able to decide whether C++ is the appropriate language for your project.

5.1 The properties of C++

C++ is not the product of a particular company but a standard which has been defined in a similar way to how, for instance, one would define the shape and characteristics of an electric socket. In the first place this means that there is a large number of different C++ compilers produced by the most diverse companies for the most diverse operating systems. On the other hand this generalizing effect means that C++ cannot reap the benefits of a specific operating system as a basic language component. This is the reason why the language definition describes only the available core functions together with an expandable framework for structuring programs. For all other properties such as graphical output, data bank access or network communication separate libraries have to be brought in. This is no fault of the language but a tribute to the fact that C++ can be used in a large variety of different environments. Since C++ is not limited to specific hardware the language is always up-to-date and can be used in any environment.

In its developed form C++ treads a fine line between efficiency and a tendency towards abstraction. Before C++ arrived there were machine-level languages on the one hand which afforded access to bits and bytes and delivered very fast programs. On the other hand there were high-level languages with powerful and clearly defined language resources which spared the user the necessity of counting bits, but which took correspondingly longer to execute. C++ uniquely manages to combine the best of both worlds. With C++ you can manipulate memory directly if you want, or you can equally well rely on commercial software which is as easy to use as a television set. Even if you write your classes yourself they may be as efficient as if they had been written in a machine-level language. It is this very search for the ideal which makes up the major part of C++ programming, but it also contributes to the appeal of the language. In order to achieve the required efficiency you have to proceed with the greatest caution. You have to ask yourself honestly whether the speed of your programs justifies the expense of writing them in C++. However, if you want to write ambitious applications C++ is hard to ignore.

An important feature of the language was the designers' intention to make it suitable for large projects. When you join a number of developers to write a large program you need the wherewithal to provide you with a manageable environment. Not every developer can have read and understood every line of code. The concept of classes lends itself best to providing a protective environment within which you are not bothered by too many details but which guarantees you access to a host of useful functions. And when immersed in a large project it's important that you should be able to find quickly the place in the code where a certain function is defined. Here too classes are a big help, since they divide the whole namespace into convenient sections. Classes which have already been written and tested are particularly productive when they are reused several times. This only occurs in reasonably large projects, but you are unlikely to learn to appreciate all of these merits by writing a small program which perhaps only copies a couple of files. You probably find it unnecessarily complicated even to define a class for this purpose, and you are probably right. It's only a thousand lines later and after the first couple of modifications that the merits of C++ become obvious.

> **Tip** C++ comes into its own when you are writing large well-structured programs.

Although this is not explicitly stated in the standard, C++ is a compiled language, not an interpreted language. This means that a compiler compiles your program into binary code. At run time no other program has to be executed. However, since the binary code has been created for a particular machine it cannot be executed on a computer with a different hardware architecture or a different operating system. In order to get your program to run on another computer you have to recompile the source code on this machine. In contrast to many other languages C++ has been so carefully standardized that the compilers are virtually interchangeable. Potential compilation problems are more likely to stem from the elements of freedom which the standard itself incorporates. An `int` or a `double`, for instance, does not occupy the same number of bits on all computers. In order to port your code successfully you have to deal with the effects of this difference. The other thing you have to ensure is that any class libraries you may use are available for the other computer. And of course your programs must not directly access an operating system's functions even though they are to be compiled in a different operating system. Within these limits C++ is portable. For example it is possible to swap one Windows version for another reasonably cheaply. Transferring from one Linux kernel to the next is purely a matter of routine.

> **Tip** C++ source code is portable within certain limits, but compiled programs cannot be run on different hardware.

There are a whole number of programming languages or dialects which have been specially designed to afford access to the functions of a particular operating system or of some other product. Thus many data banks possess an integrated basic interpreter which can be used to make high-speed connections between graphic environments and data banks. C++ cannot compete directly with these languages owing to its generalized scope. Consequently C++ is not restricted to a specific range of tasks or a specific environment. If you want instant success in a specialized area of computing with C++ you should definitely use a development environment for that particular area. These are available for a wide variety of applications. You will find using a product incorporating a special language is very cost-effective. You will also certainly benefit from the fact that many of the products or operating systems you may use in support are themselves written in C++ or C, and so the interfaces will be compatible with your own code.

Now you can begin to appreciate when and where C++ can be used with profit. To summarize we can say that C++ is not always easy to program and does not bring instant success, but that it is indispensable wherever robust and efficient programs are required. C++ is a language for professionals.

Part I

Take that!

This main section of the book describes the language resources which have not yet been covered in the first part. Part II offers more than a simple list of missing keywords; it explains how the language as a whole complex system can develop from a series of individual concepts to an effective tool for a major project.

The key to success is attention to detail. If the individual elements are used properly taking their characteristics into account, they will fit together almost automatically and operate smoothly like cogwheels. They should, however, never be used in a way that was not intended. Something that produces a time difference of a few minutes in a simple test program can easily lead to scheduling difficulties in a complex development project. The explanations are therefore often accompanied by reminders to refrain from experimenting and to observe the pragmatic procedure. This also includes a completely subjective assessment of language resources and their relevance on a daily basis. Some of the concepts of C++ were developed a long time ago and are out-dated or simply too complicated to be really useful.

Above all you should resist the temptation to experiment. During the learning phase, you should be content with trying out the things that are within reach. There is no limit to the range of possibilities for combining the different language resources.

References

6.1 References instead of pointers

Good C++ programs never use pointers.
The idea of pointers pointing at the wrong memory location is too much to bear.
Instead C++ has a related variable type which indeed itself refers to another variable, but the risk of its being misdirected is virtually non-existent. It is called a reference and is represented by the ampersand &. By analogy with a pointer to a character char*, a reference to a character is written char&. The general scope of the two types becomes clear in the following lines.

```
char charact = 'c';
char* charactPtr = &charact; // Pointer to character
char& charactRef = charact;  // Reference to character
```

In order to prevent references being misdirected they are subject to a variety of special conditions which distinguish them from pointers.

1   When a reference is instantiated the object to which it is to point must be defined.

2   A reference cannot be modified to make it point to a different object from that originally assigned.

3   There is no value for non-directional references corresponding to NULL for pointers.

To make the rules more manageable there is no de-referencing operator like the * for pointers. There is likewise no need to reference variables if you want to assign them to references. This is clear from the assignment of charact to charactRef in which no & operator precedes charact. Nevertheless there is no danger of confusing a reference with a value since one never finds oneself in the embarrassing position of redirecting a reference to itself like a pointer.

That's enough theorizing. Let's look at a couple of examples. The first shows the assignment of the contents of a pointer and the contents of a reference to a simple variable.

```
char otherCharact;
otherCharact = *charactPtr;
otherCharact = charactRef;   // Not de-referenced
```

The following statements violate the principle that references always have to be properly directed, and they are consequently not accepted by the compiler.

```
// Without assignment, will not compile!
int& numRef1;
// Non-directional, will not compile!
float& numRef2 = NULL;
```

The pointer-like effect of references nevertheless comes through to some extent. The value of reference `numRef` changes in the next few lines even though it is not directly modified.

```
int num = 100;
int& numRef = num;     // Directed, therefore OK
cout << numRef << endl; // Outputs 100
num = 33;
cout << numRef << endl; // Outputs 33
```

6.2 References as method parameters

6.2.1   Important properties

The examples we have seen hitherto do indeed demonstrate the way references function, but they are not typical of how they are used. As a rule references are used only as method parameters, and they are particularly popular used as method parameters which are objects and have no elementary type.

At this point we find ourselves in something of a quandary. If we want to examine the function of references under realistic conditions we have to assume that self-defined objects behave themselves when assigned. So our `Text` class from the first part of the book would have to cope easily with the statements

```
Text a("Cinema");
Text b("Circus");
b = a;    // Problematic
```

Unfortunately this is not the case. We need in addition a special method called an assignment operator. In order to define assignment operators properly we need to know all about references, and so we find ourselves going round and round in circles. Therefore please trust us when we say that there is a way defining assignment for objects which fits in with our experience of elementary variables. We shall explain in some detail in Chapter 8, Section 8.2 how this happens. Just assume for the moment that the Text class, which is used to represent any other self-defined object, has this well-defined assignment behavior. And now we can continue to deal with references.

When you link a reference to a variable to a method the variable is not copied but merely passed on. The variable inside the method is only another name for the parameter passed from outside.

```
void increment (int& num) {
  num++;
}
...
int val = 40;
cout << val << endl; // Outputs 40
increment (val);
cout << val << endl; // Outputs 41
```

Now we are in a position to implement the exchange function which was beyond us in Part I.

```
void exchange (int& a, int& b) {
  int temp = a; // Temporary variable
  a = b;
  b = temp;
}
...
int num1 = 56;
int num2 = 111;
exchange (num1, num2);
cout << num1 << " " << num2 << endl;
```

Success at last! The output is

```
111 56
```

and not the other way round.

Uniquely and bizarrely method calls pose the risk of references being misdirected despite all precautions. If you use references as return values of methods you must make sure that the returned object is not defined locally in the method.

```
Text& getCountry () {
  Text country ("Australia");
  return country;
}
```

The return value of this method is a reference which points into thin air, since the variable country ceases to exist at the end of the function call. Accessing the return value will result in the program crashing as surely as hitting a NULL pointer.

> **Warning** Returning a local object from a method as reference will cause a program to crash.

References are often used in parameter lists in combination with a const keyword to prevent the parameter being changed as in the example below.

```
void setText (const Text& text)
```

C++ syntax permits any combination of const and references in parameter lists, but some make little sense and belong on the margins of programming. We shall therefore start by going over all the reasons for using references and all the meanings of const. Then all that remains is to cite the handful of combinations which you really need. We'll begin with the reasons for using references.

The totality of method name, list of parameter types and return type together with its const property is incidentally known as a method's signature. If two methods in all these values coincide we say that their signature is identical.

6.2.2   References as passed parameters

References are used when parameters are passed mainly to avoid copy operations. Copy operations are among the most costly of all, especially if large quantities of data are involved, or if the same data is recopied too many times.

```
Text tomSawyer ("Tom. Tom! Aunt Polly ... ");
DisplayinWindow (tomSawyer);
```

The method DisplayinWindow does not have to create a copy of the novel *Tom Sawyer* in order to reproduce it. All that is needed is for tomSawyer to be passed as a reference.

```
void DisplayinWindow (Text& text);
```

Small parameters, on the other hand, are not as a rule passed as a reference, but as a value. This implies a simple assessment of what is more costly to copy: the variable itself or a reference to the variable. Elementary types such as `int`, `double` or `char` are nearly as large as references. Thus you will gain little by using references for elementary types.

```
void DisplayinWindow (int num);
```

The only exceptions are methods which employ a reference not to prevent copy operations but to manipulate variables from the calling program. The `exchange` method from the previous section is a method of this type. Although it is indeed useful you should try to avoid such constructs. Our notions of what to expect from a method are belied when it changes our variables via its parameters. What are we to think of a method such as

```
void DisplayinWindow (int& num);
```

when it first multiplies the passed variable in the calling program by ten and then halves it?

Even if you wish to return several values from a method you should not use a reference parameter. A method `DisplayinWindow` which reports both the success of your call and the time it takes to make could be written with a genuine return value and a reference parameter.

```
bool DisplayinWindow (int& num, int& milliseconds)
```

It would be better, however, to combine both return values in one class and return them directly. This procedure is described in Chapter 12, Section 12.3.

This is the position then:

> **Tip** Only large objects are passed to a method as reference parameters.

6.2.3   References as return values

The situation is a similar one as far as return values are concerned. Again if anything only large objects should be returned as reference. The method

```
Text& methodReference ();
```

saves a copy operation compared to

```
Text methodCopy ();
```

It is nevertheless alarming how often copy operations still occur when one of the methods is used. Let's start with the method without a reference return value. The second of the lines

```
Text text ("ABC");
Text = methodCopy ();
```

contains two copy operations by a text variable, not including the additional internal copy operations which `methodCopy` may undertake. The first copy is created when the return value, which is passed by `methodCopy` via `return`, is copied into a nameless temporary variable. This always happens when variables are not passed as references. The second copy is employed to assign the temporary variable to the variable `text`.

In the statement

```
text = methodReference ();
```

in `methodReference` the copy operation to a temporary variable is missing.

The returned reference is directly copied to the variable `text`. Needless to say it is copied only once.

We ought now to explain finally the correct way of implementing reference return values. Return values in the form of references can function only if they point to attributes of the object called or to global variables. `get` methods are good examples of the first option. They have the sole aim of gaining public access to a private attribute.

```
class Person {
public:
  text& getForename () {
    return aForename;
  }
  ...
private:
  text aForename;
  ...
};
```

The attribute `aForename` survives even after `getForename` is called, and it survives as long as the object survives. This is why the return value of the method can be a reference. It's quite safe to use a statement of the kind

```
Person person1 (...);
Text forename ("");
forename = person1.getForename ();
```

The referenced object exists at assignment time in any case, what happens to it afterwards is not your concern. By now you will be dealing with a copy.

It's more risky trying to assign the result of `getForename` to a `Text` reference in order to save the final copy. As soon as the `Person` object is destroyed, the name attribute of this object disappears too and the reference ends up pointing at nothing. We shall use a dynamically created object to test this situation. Only in this way can we call its destructor directly.

```
Person* personPtr = new Person (...);
Text& nameRef = personPtr->getForename ();
cout << nameRef << endl;  // OK
delete personPtr;  // Referenced object is destroyed.
cout << nameRef << endl;  // Probable crash.
```

Since this procedure is so risky, you have no alternative but to make a copy when returning values of methods and using a genuine variable with which to pick up the return value.

As we have already mentioned, references can also be returned to global variables instead of to attributes. This does not happen often in fact since one tries to avoid global variables whenever possible, but there is no danger of a misdirected reference.

If you cannot find a way of formulating the returned value as a reference to a surviving object your only option is to return it via a value. This is when the second copy operation we have described becomes necessary.

```
TimeOfDay createTimeOfDay (int hours, int minutes) {
  TimeOfDay timeOfDay (hours, minutes);
  return timeOfDay;
}
```

> **Tip** Only large objects are returned as references of a method, and this happens precisely where there is a possibility of formulating the return value as reference to a surviving object.

You must not take what has just been said as meaning that reference return values are generally more vulnerable than copied return values.

6.2.4   *const in method signatures*

We have explained the motives for using reference parameters and the limitations of their use. Now we have to find out when we need the const keyword. The keyword const occurs in method signatures in three different forms, all of which reflect the unchanging nature of certain variables. These forms are invariable parameters, invariable return values and methods which leave the object unchanged.

A method parameter labeled const indicates that the value passed in the method is not changed. This is not just a statement of intention but a fact. The compiler keeps watch and refuses to compile programs which take no notice of the particular limitations of const.

```
void method (const int parameter1, const int& parameter2)
{
  parameter1 = 0;    // Does not compile!
  parameter2 = 0;    // Does not compile!
}
```

The sole effect of the const keyword attached to parameter1 is to make the variable parameter1 within the method incapable of being modified, but the const keyword attached to parameter2 also affects the calling program. Since the second parameter was passed as reference, parameter2 is just another name for a variable of the calling program. If it were possible to change parameter2 within the method, the result would be that the corresponding variable in the calling program would also be changed. The const keyword therefore protects you from the unexpected side-effects of a method call – a promise to the user of the method which the compiler makes sure is kept. You are advised to use const consistently with all reference parameters which are not changed by your method. Omitting const in front of a reference parameter acts as a warning sign: this parameter will be altered by the method!

A return value which has been defined as const cannot be modified in the calling program. This principle is illustrated by the getText methods of the class ConstText below.

```
class ConstText {
public:
  ...
  Const Text& getTextConst () {
    return aText;
  }
  text& getTextNotConst () {
    return aText;
  }
```

```
private:
  Text aText;
};
```

The sole task of the class is to protect the `Text` attribute from being accessed from outside. At first sight it would appear to have acquitted itself successfully. If we use the `getText` methods of a `ConstText` object named `ct` containing `Paul` in this manner, all is well.

```
Text name1 ("");
Text name2 ("");
name1 = ct.getTextConst ();
name2 = ct.getTextNotConst ();
```

Attempting to modify the returned values will get us nowhere since we are dealing here with copies of the attribute `aText` .

```
Text otherName ("Tony");
name1 = otherName;
name2 = otherName;
```

The output we get from the lines

```
name1.output ();
name2.output ();
ct.getTextConst().output ();
```

proves this. The copies have in fact been modified, but the original has stayed the same.

```
Tony
Tony
Paul
```

If you are thinking all is well because the attribute is protected, then you are reckoning without your clever colleague sitting next to you who has pointed the return value of `getTextNotConst` to a reference. Since this reference is merely a substitute name for the referenced attribute, he is able to modify it without any difficulty.

```
Text& nameRef = ct.getTextNotConst ();
nameRef = otherName;
ct.getTextNotConst().output ();
```

Look at that! The attribute of your `ConstText` object has been modified! The original `Paul` has become `Tony`.

```
Tony
```

After this painful experience you decide to use methods such as `getTextConst` which will be too much even for your colleague. His next try

```
Text& nameRef = ct.getTextConst ();  // Does not compile!
```

will simply not compile. The compiler complains that a `const` reference is being assigned to a non-`const` reference. Another try

```
const Text& nameRef = ct.getTextConst ();
nameRef = otherName;  // Does not compile!
```

also fails, this time because it attempts to modify a `const` object.

In order to be safe for all time from mischievous attacks on your private attributes, you will do best to define reference return values always as `const`.

```
const Text& getText ();
```

The third meaning of `const` in method signatures becomes significant if we wish to prevent methods from modifying some attribute of their object. To do this we insert `const` at the end of the method signature.

```
class DisplayableText {
public:
   ...
   void DisplayinWindow () const {
      ...
      aText = Text ("Other Text"); // Does not compile!
   }
private:
   Text aText;
};
```

Whatever means `DisplayinWindow` may use to display the text in the display window, the attribute `aText` cannot be modified by the method. The compiler knows full well which are the only methods of the invariable `displayable-Text` object you are allowed to call, viz. the `const` methods, since nothing is modified by them. Let's assume for a moment that `displayableText` has at its disposal besides `DisplayinWindow` another method `add`, which is not defined as `const`. In this case the method cannot be executed for a `const` object.

```
const DisplayableText dtext =
   "Dear Aunt Clara, ...";
dtext.DisplayinWindow ();           // OK
dtext.add ("P.S. Good luck!"); // Does not compile!
```

It is true that a method declared as `const` implies limits to its implementation, but it also improves its callability. In fact many of the examples which follow in this book cannot be compiled unless we give the `output` method of `Text` the benefit of an appropriate `const` declaration.

```
class Text {
public:
  void output () const;
  ...
};
```

6.2.5   Combinations of const and references

Now that we have cast light on all the meanings of `const` we can usefully combine `const` with references.

You can see now that only reference variables have to be protected by attaching a `const` keyword. A copy of non-reference parameters is made anyway when they are passed, and this copy may modify the method in question at will without running the risk of ruining the variables of any other method.

Besides the rule that only large objects are passed as reference, there are two other practical ways of passing parameters. Here the type `int` is used to represent all elementary types. The class `Text` represents all self-defined classes, which as a rule are larger than elementary types. These are the two survivors:

```
void method (int num);
void method (const Text& text);
```

The situation as regards return values is similar.   What we have left is

```
int method ();
```

and

```
const Text& method ();
```

The second form is possible only if the returned value is either an attribute of the class to which `method` belongs or a global variable. If not then one of the two emergency solutions is brought into play.

```
Text method ();
void method (Text& text);
```

In the first case we take a chance and risk an extra copy operation. The second case guarantees that the object which receives the return value also survives the method call, since it has already been passed as a parameter. It is true that by doing this we avoid two operations as against the reference-less variant. However, we run the risk of miscalculating the significance of the parameters. The method should at least come with a heavily underlined comment to the effect that the parameter is meant to be a return value. Since this version is the most efficient of the three, many programmers accept the associated risk.

Whether the whole method should have a `const` keyword attached depends on whether it is to modify the attributes of its object. You should use `const` with any method which does not modify an attribute. But you should not rewrite your code just to attach `const` to as many methods as you can. A typical representative of the `const` method is the `get` method. It reads an attribute but does not change it. And so the method `getText` of the `ConstText` class should be accompanied by `const`.

```
const Text& getText () const {
   return aText;
}
```

Inheritance in detail

The concept of inheritance is much more diverse than the corresponding section in the introductory part might lead one to expect (Chapter 4, Section 4.6). This diversity has nothing to do with any lavish options to add to the public inheritance which has already been discussed. The high art of inheritance lies rather in restricting the features which are inherited. This is a logical continuation of the notion of encapsulation. As in real life we are often confronted with a situation in which parents will not or should not leave the whole of their property to their children. But it's not just a question of parents being mean, sometimes we have to intervene to decide which of them should do the bequeathing.

But this theme has a further surreptitious twist. All children are automatically able to show their own properties, even when addressed by their surname. Let's begin with this remarkable property of derived classes.

7.1 Polymorphism

```
class Everything {
public:
  void doWhatIMean();
};
```

This code will perhaps be used in some forty years time when the great technological problems of the age have been solved. The programming language is a remote relative of its contemporary namesake and still shows similarities of syntax to its C++ ancestor even. The class Everything refers to the scope of all that the language can deliver. Its sole method doWhatIMean does exactly what you want. Needless to say, most programmers are unemployed.

Luckily we are not there yet, but there are glimpses of that far-off time even now in some of the properties of C++. There are many situations in which the compiler can deduce from the context what is required, sparing us the need for tedious declarations.

Take for example the classes `Pair` and `Date` from the first part of the book and a third class, `TimeOfDay`, which is also derived from `Pair`. `TimeOfDay` uses both num attributes as memory locations for hours and minutes.

```
class TimeOfDay : public Pair {
public:
  // Constructor
  TimeOfDay (int hours, int minutes) {
    setNum1 (hours);
    setNum2 (minutes);
  }
  // Output method
  void output () {
    cout << getNum1 () << ":" << getNum2 ()
         << " Hours" << endl;
  }
};
```

As you can see from the code, `TimeOfDay` outputs its value in formatted form.

```
TimeOfDay fiveToTwelve (11,55);
fiveToTwelve.output ();
```

The output is

```
11:55 Hours
```

In order to accommodate all the various time values, we enter all the objects derived from `Pair` into a list in our program. The list will point to `Pair` objects and therefore has elements of the type `Pair*`.

```
Pair* list[4];
```

Next we assign different objects to each list array.

```
list[0] = new Pair (3,7);
list[1] = new Pair (2,8);
list[2] = new Date (1,1,1900);
list[3] = new TimeOfDay (16,11);
```

In fact the list arrays are pointers to `Pair`. Despite this you can easily assign a pointer to `Date` or a pointer to `TimeOfDay` without the compiler giving you any problems. As far as the compiler is concerned every `Date` object has a `Pair` object in tow since `Date` is derived from `Pair`. Both `TimeOfDay` and `Date` are simply special forms of number pairs with a few additional features.

The next thing you will want to do is program a loop which outputs all the objects in the list. You can try this using the following construct:

```
for (int i=0; i<4; i++) {
  list[i]->output();
}
```

The code compiles without errors, but it just does not output what one might expect.

```
3 7
2 8
1 1
16 11
```

This looks rather alarming: both the year element of the `Date` object and the colon in the time of day are missing. But if you check what statements the compiler received the result is more comprehensible. The list was defined as a list of pointers to `Pair` objects. If the `output` method was called for one of the objects it is only logical that the `output` method of the class `Pair` should have been called too. The latter displayed only the two attributes belonging to `Pair`. This is understandable but unsatisfactory.

The problem can be solved by a minor change in the class definition of `Pair`. We declare `output` as a virtual method

```
class Pair {
  ...
  virtual void output();
  ...
};
```

Now when we execute the loop we get the result we wanted.

```
3 7
2 8
1.1.1900
16:11
```

There's a whiff of `doWhatIMean` here. The program has realized independently which of the `output` methods is to be called, namely that of the type derived from `Pair` to which the `Pair` pointer actually points. This only works when the virtual method is accessed via a pointer to the base class. If you use the object itself instead of a pointer, the object type will be known anyway and all the magic will be completely unnecessary. The accompanying mnemonic sounds a bit crude.

Tip When an object's virtual method is called via a base class pointer the corresponding method of the derived type is executed.

The `virtual` property inherits. When a method is declared as `virtual`, only methods with the same name with an identical signature in all derived classes are affected. Other methods are untouched, even methods of the same name with different arguments. Since methods in derived classes are automatically `virtual` if their namesake is in the base class, one is easily tempted to leave out this property when defining them. Although this is syntactically correct it prevents us from observing how the method in the derived class behaves in action. For this reason you should always attach the `virtual` keyword in all derived classes.

```
class Date {
   ...
   virtual void output();
   ...
};
```

In the object-oriented world each property of a language has its fine-sounding name. Since in the last example it was possible for a `Pair` object to behave like a `Date` object or a `TimeOfDay` object depending on choice, we talk about the polymorphism of objects.

7.2 Polymorphism at work

7.2.1 An example

In the routine application of polymorphic classes we almost inevitably come across several interesting consequences of the concept, together with a couple of temptations, this time with serious consequences, to which you should not succumb. Because the examples are so graphic we are going to examine them via a class for house pets. House pets have a fairly simple routine which is mostly limited to running around and eating. The `Pet` base class addresses this fact and makes a method available for each of the two activities; virtually, of course, since they are to override the various kinds of pet with their specific type of behavior.

```
class Pet {
public:
  virtual void runAround ();
  virtual void feed ();
};
class Dog : public Pet {
public:
  // Only eats tinned food
  virtual void feed ();
};
class Cat : public Pet {
public:
  // Moves with feline grace
  virtual void runAround ();
};
class Hamster : public Pet {
};
```

The dog runs around like all the other pets. Only his eating habits are different. He refuses any food which does not come out of a tin. And so the method `feed` in the `Dog` class is initially defined. In the case of the cat we have to redefine `runAround`. She moves around much more gracefully than the other pets. The hamster is the only one of the pets without any special characteristics and so he uses the two methods from the base class.

A method which reproduces the daily routine of a pet can access both the pet's methods without any knowledge of the special sub-type.

```
void dailyRoutine (Pet* petPtr) {
  if (petPtr != NULL) {
    petPtr->runAround ();
    petPtr->feed ();
    petPtr->runAround ();
  }
}
```

Since both methods are declared as `virtual` and we access the various pets via a base class pointer, a different `feed` method is used for the dog than for the other pets.

7.2.2   Polymorphic references

In the `dailyRoutine` method we have used an `if` statement to prevent the pointer parameter assuming the value NULL. This is the only way of stopping the program crashing if we try to dereference the NULL pointer. The fact that we have used a pointer here at all flouts many of the principles proclaimed in the chapter on references such as "a good C++ program manages with hardly any pointers". Or "C++ possesses a construct related to the pointer which virtually eliminates the risk of misdirection". Very well then, let's try our luck with references.

```
void dailyRoutine (Pet& pet) {
  pet.runAround ();
  pet.feed ();
  pet.runAround ();
}
```

The query addressed to NULL can now be omitted since references cannot be non-directional. The arrows for dereferencing the pointer have been replaced by dots as is the practice for references. Whether you define the pet with const depends on whether feed and runAround modify attributes of the Pet object. The only question now is whether the method functions in the same way as before. Up till now we have seen polymorphism used only for accesses via a base class pointer. What happens now that we call the new version of dailyRoutine with a Dog object? Will the feed attached to the Dog method be called as we wanted or only the feed associated with the Pet method?

The concept of references would not justify its claims if it were not compatible with polymorphic classes. Thus accessing a virtual method via a base class reference has the same effect as accessing it via a base class pointer: the appropriate derived method is called. References and pointers, in other words, are complete equivalents as far as polymorphic classes are concerned.

Tip When an object is accessed via a base class reference the relevant derived version of a virtual method is called.

In doubtful cases the variant of dailyRoutine which uses a reference argument is to be preferred since it is less error-prone and more transparent than the pointer variant. In fact base class references are mostly used as method parameters, while base class pointers are preferred when the object in question is created in the same method. This is again related to the fact that references cannot be non-directional. If at all possible, however, you should not mix references and pointers since you will then reap the disadvantages of both concepts. In order to keep the two methods separate in the following examples we shall refer to them as dailyRoutineWithPtr and dailyRoutineWithRef.

A section of code appropriately using `dailyRoutineWithRef` creates an automatic variable for a `Pet` and calls the method.

```
Dog fido;
dailyRoutineWithRef (fido);
```

If the section of code contains only a dynamically created `Pet` object in the form of a pointer, then the `dailyRoutineWithPtr` should be preferred.

```
Dog* fidoPtr = new Dog;
dailyRoutineWithPtr (fidoPtr);
```

The two mixed forms

```
dailyRoutineWithRef (*fidoPtr);
```

and

```
dailyRoutineWithPtr (&fido);
```

are not particularly elegant. There is the underlying danger in the first form especially when the pointer is NULL or is misdirected, for which the reference method is not equipped at all. This type of call is certain to crash the program. You should decide first whether you want to use the `dailyRoutine` method with references or pointers and then implement only one of the variants. If you keep this possibility of choice at the back of your mind you will find yourself relying much less often on the pointer variant.

7.2.3   The allure of downcast

If a class hierarchy proves successful in a program there are soon calls for its expansion. This is not a problem since program code is a living entity, and the object-oriented approach prepares us for expansions. You have found that cats spend time not only running around but also scratching sofas. And so you expand the cat class by one method.

```
class Cat {
public:
  void sharpenClaws ();
  ...
};
```

Since only cats do this and you have no intention of subdividing cats any further, you have no need to declare the method `virtual`. The next step is to include the new activity in the pets' daily routine by appropriately changing the method `dailyRoutine`. We use `dailyRoutineWithPtr` in a representative capacity in order to take a shortcut to the most sensible solution, and we walk straight into the first trap.

```
void dailyRoutineWithPtr (pet* petPtr) {
  if (petPtr != NULL) {
    petPtr->runAround ();
    petPtr->feed ();
    petPtr->runAround ();
    petPtr->sharpenClaws ();   // Does not compile
  }
}
```

The method sharpenClaws is defined for cats, it's true, but not for any pets you like. And so the compiler cannot compile code which calls sharpenClaws via a Pet pointer. What we really needed was a construct which calls the method only when we are actually dealing with cats. We want a pointer to a base class object to help us work out from what derived class the object to which it is pointing emanates. The answer is a dynamic_cast. We replace the call to sharpenClaws with the following code.

```
Cat* catPtr = dynamic_cast<Cat*> (petPtr);
if (catPtr != NULL) {
    catPtr->sharpenClaws ();
}
```

The job of dynamic_cast is to test whether each pet pointer can be turned into a pointer of the type contained in the angle brackets. If this is possible the result is a pointer of the indicated type, otherwise the result is NULL. We store the return value for our purposes in a Cat* and call the cat-specific method sharpenClaws in case it differs from NULL. This is exactly what we intended.

Tip Type conversions between pointers to objects of the same class hierarchy can safely be made using dynamic_cast.

When you consider the principle behind a dynamic_cast you quickly reach the conclusion that it must do a lot more than simply reinterpret the bytes to which petPtr is pointing. It is of a far different order from a type conversion such as int and double since the work cannot be done by the compiler. At the moment of translation it is not yet apparent what sort of type will be passed to dailyRoutineWithPtr. It could be one different type after another. Therefore dynamic_cast must be evaluated at run-time, and dynamic_cast must find out from somewhere what type has actually been passed. Information like this is available only if the class in question possesses virtual methods. Otherwise the compiler does not provide any space for type information. dynamic_cast compares type information with the target type and in this way can decide whether a pointer of the desired type or `NULL` is returned. The procedure involved in the call to `dynamic_cast` is also called Run Time Type Information (RTTI).

> **Tip** `dynamic_cast` exists on the assumption that the base class possesses at least one virtual method.

Since the job of `dynamic_cast` is not that simple, its execution takes much longer than would a conversion between elementary types. If the efficiency of your program is important to you, you should use `dynamic_cast` sparingly. In fact a downcast, as it is known, i.e. a type conversion from a base class to a more special derived class, contradicts the idea of inheritance. We introduced inheritance as a way of converting common aspects of different classes into elegant code. A language element which has the sole purpose of highlighting differences between classes of the same inheritance tree has a counterproductive effect.

7.2.4   Avoiding downcasts

In fact there is a more elegant option when it comes to modeling the particular behavior of the cat. Derivation, which is part of the specialized toolkit of C++, is the correct choice for this situation. Why shouldn't we make `dailyRoutine` a method of pet? We can then lump all the pets together. If any pet steps out of line we can override the method.

```
class Pet {
public:
  virtual void runAround ();
  virtual void feed ();
  virtual void dailyRoutine ();
};
class Dog : public Pet {
public:
  virtual void feed ();
};
class Cat : public Pet {
public:
  virtual void runAround ();
  virtual void dailyRoutine ();
  void sharpenClaws ();
};
class Hamster : public Pet {
};
```

The only method implementation we are interested in is that of `dailyRoutine`. This method is initially defined in `Pet`. The `Pet` parameter has fallen by the way-side, incidentally, since the method now has direct access to such an object.

```cpp
void Pet::dailyRoutine () {
  runAround ();
  feed ();
  runAround ();
}
```

Be sure to note that in a separate method definition such as this the `virtual` attachment preceding the method name is omitted. The `.cpp` merely serves as a collection of method definitions without a class concept. It does not contain any keywords such as `virtual` with significance for the method structure of a whole class tree.

Although the code is short, what happens in the method is remarkable. The statements

```cpp
Dog rover;
rover.dailyRoutine ();
```

call the method `dailyRoutine` of dog. Since `Dog` does not have its own version of `dailyRoutine` the base class method is used. This works even though there is no `virtual` attached. It's an exciting moment when `dailyRoutine` is executed: there's a risk that the `Pet` variant of the method `feed` will be applied. Dogs have their own peculiar eating habits. This is where the `virtual` declaration of `feed` comes into its own. Method calls within a class behave polymorphically. The `feed` of `Dog` is executed and Rover, like a real dog, refuses any food which does not come out of a tin. The two calls made by `runAround` within `dailyRoutine` naturally only reach the base class variants since the methods in `Dog` are not overridden.

`dailyRoutine` works well for a dog. We can now override the method in `Cat`. Here we can make use of the scope resolution notation. Remember it? By attaching a double colon to a class name we can define which class is being accessed by a method or attribute. We shall use the scope resolution operator first of all to call the `dailyRoutine` method of the base class which executes `runAround`, `feed` and again `runAround`. As before in the case of `Dog` the variants of the called methods which really belong to `Cat` are executed. We then call the cat method `sharpenClaws`. Since this code is executed for `Cat` objects only, we have no need to worry whether or not `sharpenClaws` is defined:

```cpp
void Cat::dailyRoutine () {
  Pet::dailyRoutine ();
  sharpenClaws ();
}
```

We have now found an acceptable option for modeling the daily routines of various house pets without having to call on the rather extravagant services of `dynamic_cast`. There are, however, situations in which it makes sense to use `dynamic_cast`. This is the case when unlike the compiler we know in advance that the pointer which is to be converted is pointing to an object of the correct target type. We shall examine an example of this in Section 7.6 on Multiple inheritance.

In addition, Chapter 10, Section 10.4 includes a general survey summarizing all kinds of type conversions. It also lays the basis for a discussion of `dynamic_cast` for reference types, something which we have withheld from you so far.

7.3 The inheritance of interfaces

When we bequeath the properties of an object publicly, as we have always done in the past, the children inherit unasked all their parents' methods and attributes. This is often unnecessary baggage which they are dragging around, since they are going to override them anyway. Sometimes even when you are writing a base class you are not bothered about how the various methods might be programmed but just want to make sure that they are there in the program. Or, to carry the idea to extremes, sometimes the base class just describes an abstract concept which is never needed as a concrete object in your program. A much-used example of this state of affairs is a class hierarchy of different vehicles. Classes for ships, cars and airplanes are derived from a base class `Vehicle`. If your program is to describe the movement of individual vehicles you will not embarrass yourself by creating a base class `Vehicle`. Each object you move is either a ship, a car or an airplane.

The construct which models this relationship in C++ is the abstract base class. It is never instantiated itself. Instead it just determines which methods your subclasses have to define.

```
class Vehicle {
public:
  virtual void setTarget(const Text& target) = 0;
  virtual void moveOff () = 0;
  virtual void stop () = 0;
};
```

There is no special keyword for indicating that the base class is abstract in nature. All you have to do is define at least one of the methods as a pure virtual method by the addition of `= 0`. This means that there is no means of implementing the method in this class. The class is therefore an abstract class.

Tip Pure virtual methods have no implementation. A class with at least one pure virtual method is an abstract base class.

How should an object of the class respond when one of the pure virtual methods is called? It cannot respond, in fact, because there is no way of knowing in the class what the relevant method is doing. Therefore this class must not be instantiated. Even so it's not valueless, after all it defines which methods the derived classes have to implement to become concrete. This also explains why only virtual methods can be purely virtual. In the case of other methods one cannot provide a definition in a derived class.

A concrete class derived from `Vehicle` ought to contain the following definitions at least.

```
class Airplane : public Vehicle {
public:
  virtual void setTarget (const Text& target) {
    // Set target
  }
  virtual void moveOff () {
    // moveOff
  }
  virtual void stop () {
    // Stop
  }
};
```

Abstract base classes are occasionally a great help if we want to impose on several completely different objects a property which is common in only one respect. If, for example, we were defining a class for lists of certain objects we would want to give them for future use at least the property of being a list element. List elements must know what precedes and what succeeds them. Furthermore our list elements will generate a characteristic numerical value for sorting purposes. Each class can decide for itself how this numerical is defined from their attributes.

```
class ListElement {
public:
  ListElement* precursorPtr;
  ListElement* successorPtr;
  virtual int getSortValue() = 0;
};
```

With this abstract base class we can define any type of list element we like which has its distinctive independent properties.

This may be a pair of numbers suitable for listing, for example, which can also be sorted according to the product of the two numbers.

```
class PairElement : public ListElement {
public:
  ...
  virtual int getSortValue () {
    return aNum1*aNum2;
  }
private:
  int aNum1;
  int aNum2;
};
```

Or it may be a text class suitable for listing which can be sorted according to initial letters. Empty texts are sorted to the back.

```
class TextElement : public ListElement {
public:
  ...
  virtual int getSortValue () {
    if (aTextPtr == NULL) {
      return 256;          // Highest possible value
    }
    else {
      return (int)*aTextPtr;
    }
  }
private:
  char* aTextPtr;
};
```

In both examples the classes which have been derived from the abstract base class have inherited just the interfaces and not the implementation of the individual methods.

> **Tip** Derivation from an abstract base class means inheriting the interface but not an implementation.

Since the list class we have merely mentioned up till now will be equally suitable as an illustrative object, we shall give a brief outline of it as a whole. It possesses three attributes of a pointer which point to the first, the last and the current list element. It also has methods for adding list elements, determining the next list element, redirecting the list pointer to the start and sorting the list as a whole.

```
class List {
public:
  List ();
  void insert (ListElement* elementPtr);
  ListElement* nextElement ();
  void redirect ();
  void sort ();
private:
  ListElement* aStartPtr;
  ListElement* aEndPtr;
  ListElement* aCurrentPtr;
};
```

The class makes a lot of use of the signaling effect of NULL pointers. Thus all pointers to which no definite list element has yet been assigned have a NULL attached. Also the method nextElement returns NULL if no next element exists. The following is an example of how all the elements of a list can be read:

```
list.redirect ();
ListElement* lePtr = NULL;
for (lePtr = list.nextElement (); lePtr != NULL;
     lePtr = list.nextElement ())
{
  // Use lePtr
}
```

7.4 Private inheritance

Instead of the public attachment you can also use the keyword private when declaring a derived class. By doing so you stop the methods and attributes which were public in the base class from being accessed by other classes. The private methods and attributes of the base class are inaccessible from outside anyway. Now as before, the derived class can access the public properties of the base class. private properties are inaccessible to the derived class in the case of public inheritance as well.

All read and inwardly digested? Then you should have no problem with the examples. The class Base has both a public and a private attribute and method.

The classes `PublicDerived` and `PrivateDerived` are derived from the base class `Base` and are called – would you believe – `public` and `private`.

```cpp
class Base {
public:
  void method1 ();
  int attribute1;
private:
  void method2 ();
  int attribute2;
};
class PublicDerived : public Base {
public:
  void method ();
};
class PrivatelyDerived: private Base {
public:
  void method ();
};
```

With the method definitions of the two derived classes we can first check that there is no difference internally between `private` inheritance and `public` inheritance.

```cpp
void PublicDerived::method () {
  // Use public properties of the Base class
  method1 ();
  attribute1 = 10;
  // Use private properties of the Base class
  method2 ();       // Does not compile!
  attribute2 = 10;  // Does not compile!
}
void PrivatelyDerived::method () {
  // Use public properties of the Base class
  method1 ();
  attribute1 = 10;
  // Use private properties of the Base class
  method2 ();       // Does not compile!
  attribute2 = 10; // Does not compile!
}
```

If we try to call the inherited methods from outside, the difference between the two types of inheritance becomes clear. The public methods of the base class cannot be called via the privately derived class.

```
PublicDerived pub;
pub.method1 ();
pub.attribute1 = 10;
PrivateDerived priv;
priv.method1();        // Does not compile!
priv.attribute1 = 10;  // Does not compile!
```

Of course the private attributes and methods of the base class cannot be addressed via the derived class either.

So much for the technical effects of private inheritance. What then is the real significance of this operation? Since base class methods are not accessible via the derived class there can be no question of the base class interface being inherited. However, base class methods can be very happily used internally by the derived class. The whole inheritance process would be pointless if the derived class did not at least itself make use of inherited methods. We are therefore justified in stating that the implementation of the base class was inherited.

> **Tip** Private inheritance means inheriting the implementation but not the interface.

The triad of inheritance options is now complete. The two others were public inheritance and inheritance from an abstract base class. Public inheritance is inheritance of implementation and interface. Inheritance from an abstract base class is inheritance of interface without implementation.

A note about `private` properties in general, since it is so easy to slip up here. An object's private methods and attributes are inaccessible to other classes but not to other objects of the same class. A private method `private` of `ClassA` cannot be called in a method of an object of `ClassB` or in the `main` function.

```
main () {
  ClassA a;
  a.private();   // Does not compile!
}
```

In method `method` of `ClassA` the `private` method of a different object from `ClassA` can be executed without any problem.

```
void ClassA::method (ClassA a) {
  a.private ();  // OK
}
```

7.5 Protected and friend elements

We have all the mechanisms at our command that we need to determine for a whole class which base class elements are available to it internally and externally. This is controlled by private and public inheritance. At the same time we can also determine for individual methods and attributes how visible they are. For this we need only to interpose them between the `private` and `public` sections of the class definition. Both sections, by the way, can be interchanged within a class as often as you like.

The next adaptation concerns the `protected` keyword. When we mark a section of the class definition with `protected`, we are stipulating that the methods and attributes defined there are to be visible only to the derived class. Other classes have no access to `protected` properties. In the example the base class contains methods of all grades of visibility. The rules for the visibility of attributes are identical to those of methods.

```
class Base {
public:
  void methodPublic ();
protected:
  void methodProtected ();
private:
  void methodPrivate ();
};
class Derived : public Base {
  void method ();
};
```

With these class definitions we can examine all the situations which are of interest to us. Outside only the `public` method of the base class is visible.

```
Derived derived;
derived.methodPublic ();     // OK
derived.methodProtected ();  // Does not compile!
derived.methodPrivate ();    // Does not compile!
```

Internally, however, methods of the derived class can perfectly well use the `protected` method of the base class. The truth of this is evident in the declaration of `method` in the derived class.

```
void Derived::method () {
  methodPublic ();      // OK
  methodProtected ();   // Also OK!
  methodPrivate ();     // Does not compile!
}
```

Base class attributes and methods labeled `protected` can be used only by a derived class and not by an alien class.

At this point our discussion turns to another aspect of the question with the introduction of `friend` classes. Should it not be possible for a class to allow a certain other class to access its private properties? In C++ the answer is yes, but permission is granted in one direction only. The alien class cannot decide to look at the original class's private data, the original class has to allow it first.

```
class OneClass {
friend class AnotherClass;  // Permission granted
private:
  int attribute;
  void method ();
};
class AnotherClass {
  void method (OneClass obj) {
    obj.attribute = 10; // OK, compiles
    obj.method ();      // OK, compiles
  }
};
```

Private attributes and methods of `OneClass` can be used in a method of `AnotherClass` without a peep from the compiler.

Tip By means of a `friend` declaration one class can make all of its private attributes and methods accessible to a specific other class.

Do not underestimate the power of a `friend` relationship. It binds two classes together more strongly than derivation. As we have just learned, derived classes can use a base class's `protected` methods and attributes and the public ones as well. `friend` classes can even manipulate private attributes of the befriended class, undermining the concept of object encapsulation. Therefore purists and the specialists condemn this construct, but for mere mortals it can occasionally be just what is needed at a particular time. We can use it to remove an unwanted class limit without endangering the encapsulation of the classes in question vis-à-vis other classes or rebuilding the whole derivation structure. Nevertheless you should use `friend` relationships sparingly, since they too easily become an excuse for a quick demolition operation. You can be looking at somebody else's program and wondering why for no apparent reason it modifies another class's attributes, and then it finally hits you that there's a `friend` at work here. If you find yourself faced with the need to erase the limits between two classes, you might ask yourself whether it would not be better to combine them both in a single class.

7.6 Multiple inheritance

7.6.1   Independent base classes

In the list example in Section 7.3 on abstract base classes we rewrote the class `Pair` and gave it another name in order to be able to derive it from `ListElement`. By doing this we obtained a list element which simultaneously stores pairs of numbers. The fact that the program code which we had just created was rewritten will seem odd to some. In fact we could have achieved the same result more simply. The inheritance concept does not stop us deriving one class from two or more other classes.

```
class PairAndElement : public Pair, public ListElement {
public:
  virtual int getSortValue () {
    return getNum1 () * getNum2 ();
  }
};
```

`PairAndElement` is derived from both `Pair` and `ListElement`. Since `ListElement` is abstract, `PairAndElement` must define the method `getSortValue` for it to be capable of instantiation. You can see that the rules for simple inheritance are equally valid for multiple inheritance. The best thing about all this is – it works! In less than ten lines we have created a class which both uses our tried and tested code for number pairs and also behaves like a list element. When we modify the `Pair` class we need only recompile the class `PairAndElement` and it is up to date.

There are a couple of minor limitations which should not deprive us of the pleasure of multiple inheritance in this form.

You must not define the same virtual methods in both base classes. Which of them should be executed when you call them with a `PairAndElement` object? Luckily it's relatively unlikely that two method names will collide if the classes have different tasks to perform. Anyway we would be told that this has happened by the compiler.

The second limitation concerns the clarity of pointers pointing to a `PairAndElement` object. Each `PairAndElement` is at the same time a special form of `Pair`. We can therefore let a `Pair` pointer point to a `PairAndElement`.

```
PairAndElement a;
Pair* pairPtr = &a;
```

The same applies to a `ListElement` pointer.

```
ListElement* elementPtr = &a;
```

We are not in a position to make conjectures about how the compiler saves objects to main memory. We have to accept the fact that everything not regulated by the standard will be arbitrarily handled by one or the other compiler. We write our programs for some standard C++ compiler, not for a special version of compiler from a specific manufacturer. This being the case we have no guarantee from the standard that `pairPtr` is the same as `elementPtr`. Mostly we do not mind since as a rule we use base class pointers to call a method. The method is found in spite of the ambiguous nature of the pointer. The only time we have to be on our guard is when we want to test two objects for identity using their addresses.

Now that we have assumed that the two base classes perform completely different tasks, and in particular that they have no other common base class, the likelihood of unintentionally sliding into a comparable unpleasant situation is a small one. Until the moment when we hit upon the idea of deriving them simultaneously both base classes belonged to strictly separate conceptual worlds. Methods which use a `ListElement` pointer have no reason to assume that this pointer could be connected in any way with the `Pair` class, and vice-versa. To compare the two would be like comparing apples with pears. With a little discipline we can succeed in keeping the different worlds apart even after multiple inheritance. There is nothing to stop the list class, for example, defining a method

TAKE THAT!

```
bool contains (const ListElement* elementPtr)
```

which states whether a certain element is one of the contents of the list. It is clear from the context and the method signature that the `ListElement` base class is meant.

The time has now come to fetch `dynamic_cast` out from its hidey-hole. We gave it a brief outing in order to perform safe conversions from one base class pointer to a pointer to a derived class. We soon decided that it should not be used quite so unreservedly because it seemed that we were proceeding against the spirit of inheritance. The situation we are in here is quite different however. This time we are not going down a level in the class hierarchy but round the corner, as it were, on the same derivation level. This is always necessary when we transfer an object to its specific role from its role as a list element.

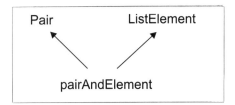

Figure 7.1   *The derivation tree of pairAndElement*

A situation like this exists in the case of the method `nextElement` of the list class which returns a pointer to an element.

```
ListElement* nextElement ();
```

In order to employ the `ListElement` pointer profitably we shall change it into a `PairAndElement` pointer, see Figure 7.1. We are sure that we have previously added only objects of the type `PairAndElement` to the list. Or are we? We can only find out for certain by testing with `dynamic_cast`.

```
ListElement* elementPtr = list.nextElement ();
Pair* pairPtr = dynamic_cast<Pair*> (elementPtr);
if (pairPtr != NULL) {
   pairPtr->output ();
}
else {
  // We must have made some mistake.
}
```

The whole thing functions under the proviso that the classes involved possess virtual methods. Only then will the information be embedded in the objects which are needed to check at run time the object type that is actually preceded by a base class.

7.6.2　The diamond constellation

Multiple inheritance is much more problematical if both base classes are derived from another common base class.

In order to investigate the dangers presented by the multiple inheritance of classes with a common base class we shall have a look at the concept of the air automobile, an invention which has come to naught so far. Most air automobile projects have failed in the simulation phase, which was implemented with C++ programs. To remind you, here is the vehicles' derivation hierarchy in shorthand form.

```
class Vehicle {
  . . .
};
class Airplane : public Vehicle {
  . . .
};
class Car : public Vehicle {
  . . .
};
```

After the positive experiences we have had with list elements it would seem reasonable to declare the air automobile as follows.

```
class Aircar : public Airplane, public Car {
  . . .
};
```

And already you have bought yourself a stack of problems which can involve you in hours of debugging sessions!

We shall try to define a `Vehicle` pointer pointing to an `Aircar`. We are allowed to do this since each `Aircar` is a special kind of `Vehicle`. There are two ways of getting to this pointer. The first involves explicitly converting the `Aircar` pointer into a `Car` pointer and then accessing the `Vehicle` component of the car component of the `Aircar`. Phew!

```
Vehicle* vehiclePtr1 = (Car*) &aircar;
```

The other way is to get a pointer to the `Vehicle` component of the air automobile by taking a shortcut via an `Airplane` pointer.

```
Vehicle* vehiclePtr2 = (Airplane*) &aircar;
```

Here it is quite clear that the two pointers `vehiclePtr1` and `vehiclePtr2` cannot be identical. They are pointers to two different objects: on the one hand the `Vehicle` component of an airplane and on the other the `Vehicle` component of a car. Again we have a problem with the clarity of objects: `vehiclePtr1` and `vehiclePtr2` are actually pointing to the same `Aircar` object. And we have already written a number of methods which function with `Vehicle` pointers, otherwise we would not have needed the common base class at all. Here we felt the full weight of the problem of clarity.

And we have exactly the same scenario with colliding method names. What appeared unlikely in the case of `Pair` and `ListElement`, namely that both define a method with the same name and the same list of parameters, is in this case preprogrammed. `Airplane` and `Car` very probably redefine a virtual method of `Vehicle`. In fact they have to in case `Vehicle` possesses a pure virtual method. Which of the two methods should be executed then if we address `Aircar` via a `Vehicle` pointer?

`dynamic_cast` also has its problems if we do not tell it which path it is to take on its search for a base class. It still works though when we summon it for conversion into a `Car` pointer.

```
Aircar* aircarPtr = &aircar;
Car* autoPtr = dynamic_cast<Car*> (aircarPtr);
if (autoPtr != NULL) {
   Vehicle* vehiclePtr1 = autoPtr;
}
```

Here we are converting an `Aircar` pointer directly into a `Vehicle` pointer. Since this statement is not unambiguous, `dynamic_cast` always returns `NULL`. In certain circumstances this code cannot even be compiled.

```
Aircar* aircarPtr = &aircar;
Vehicle* vehiclePtr =
  dynamic_cast<Vehicle*> (aircarPtr);
if (vehiclePtr != NULL) {
   // Is not reached.
}
```

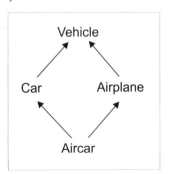

Figure 7.2 *The diamond-shaped derivation hierarchy of aircar*

The configuration described above in which a class is derived from two other classes with a common base class is called a diamond constellation. The graph showing the derivation of the vehicle classes makes it clear why, see Figure 7.2. The problems we run into with diamond-shaped derivation hierarchies outweigh by far the saving in code. The only answer is to steer clear of this constellation as far as possible.

However, this should not stop you implementing multiple inheritance from completely independent classes. If two methods of base classes should inadvertently be given the same names the compiler will tell you. Despite the slight snag multiple inheritance under these conditions is well worth the undertaking.

7.6.3   Virtual base classes

Virtual base classes are a language resource which minimizes the risks of diamond-shaped inheritance. Even when they fulfill this criterion what we said in the previous section about diamond-shaped multiple inheritance remains valid in principle.

The problem about the diamond constellation was that an object of the most remotely derived class contains more than one specimen of the first base class. For instance `Aircar` contains two different vehicle objects. If we designate the derivation of the classes `Car` and `Airplane` from `Vehicle` as `Virtual`, the `Vehicle` object of an aircar becomes unambiguous.

```
class Vehicle {
   ...
};
class Airplane : public virtual Vehicle {
   ...
};
class Car : public virtual Vehicle {
   ...
};
class Aircar : public Airplane, public Car {
   ...
};
```

Now both vehicle pointers point to the same `Vehicle` object:

```
Car* carPtr = dynamic_cast<Car*> (&aircar);
if (carPtr != NULL) {
   Vehicle* vehiclePtr1 = autoPtr;
}
```

and

```
Airplane* airplanePtr =
  dynamic_cast<Airplane*> (&aircar);
if (airplanePtr != NULL) {
   Vehicle* vehiclePtr2 = airplanePtr;
}
```

and are therefore the same.

> **Tip** Every object of a class with a virtual base class contains exactly one object of this base class.

Now even a direct conversion from an `Aircar` pointer into a `Vehicle` pointer is successful.

```
Vehicle* vehiclePtr =
  dynamic_cast<Vehicle*> (&aircar);
if (vehiclePtr != NULL) {
   // Is reached.
}
```

The main criticism directed at diamond-shaped inheritance in the previous section was not that base class pointers were ambiguous or that methods of the same name might collide. This is also the case in simple multiple inheritance and likewise in the diamonds created by virtual inheritance. The problem was rather that in diamond-shaped inheritance you are much more likely to use code which is susceptible to the two sources of error. The code is at risk even before the diamond is completed by the final virtual inheritance step. This criticism still applies if you summon the help of virtual base classes.

7.7 Objects as attributes

Part of the high art of inheritance is not to inherit if you don't have to. Two classes can relate to each other more simply and perhaps more transparently than in a derived relationship. One class can just use an object of the other class as an attribute. We tried out one such constellation without much fuss in the declaration of the `Person` class.

```
class Person {
  ...
private:
  Text aForename;
  Text aSurname;
};
```

The attributes `aForename` and `aSurname` are themselves objects, but it does not occur to us to derive `Person` from the class `Text`. This is because the relationship between the different objects in this example is so obvious. When you model more abstract objects in classes you are more likely to have to decide whether to inherit or aggregate, as the procedure is called. In order to make the decision easier for you here are a couple of rules of thumb.

Public inheritance is a particularization of the base class. A car is a particular kind of vehicle. On the other hand it is absurd to say that a person could be a particular kind of text. Inheritance is typically implemented from a single base class. Aggregation often uses several attribute classes, sometimes even identical ones.

Aggregation gives excellent service, especially when the higher-order class needs its attribute only occasionally. In order to avoid occupying unnecessary memory you just define a pointer attribute which is initially unoccupied. The object in question is not committed to memory until it turns out that it is really needed. With inheritance you do not have this option of simply switching on or off part of the object.

To demonstrate this we are going to examine the case of an attribute in the `Person` class in which information about a rucksack can be stored together with its contents. Since the person does not always carry a rucksack, and a rucksack filled to the brim takes up a lot of memory, we shall use a pointer attribute.

```
class Person {
  ...
private:
  Text aForename;
  Text aSurname;
  Rucksack* aRucksackPtr;
};
```

In the constructor we can set the `Rucksack` pointer to point to `NULL` and thereby use up no memory. The pointer attribute is occupied, either by a deep copy or a flat one as here, only when the person puts the rucksack on.

```
void putOn (Rucksack* rucksackPtr) {
  aRucksackPtr = rucksackPtr;
}
```

The counterpart to this, defined below, is a method for taking the rucksack off. It has to free the memory occupied by the rucksack.

```
void takeOff () {
  delete aRucksackPtr;
  aRucksackPtr = NULL;
}
```

It is most important that `takeOff` sets the pointer to point to `NULL`, otherwise the `delete` in the destructor would not know whether there is something to free.

```
~Person () {
  delete aRucksackPtr;
}
```

The rucksack example is representative of all constellations in which an object only occasionally has another complex object at its disposal. Had we tried to force `Person` and `Rucksack` despite the difference in meaning into an inheritance relationship, each person would have occupied a rucksack's memory location.

Methods in detail

The most important components of a program are the methods. They control the dynamic behavior of objects. Without methods, classes would be useless graveyards for data. No wonder, then, that C++ provides a whole range of useful notations for method calls which make your code easier to understand.

We take advantage of the fact that each new class generates a need for methods with specific tasks. This enables us to implement these methods uniformly and to examine the potential merits and risks of examples of a large number of similar methods. One of the most popular is the assignment operator introduced in Chapter 6 on references.

The present chapter also describes how we can supply method parameters with typical values which do not then have to be redefined when called. We also gather another clutch of constructors and destructors. And finally, we have a look at the fast movers among methods, inline methods.

8.1 Constructors and destructors

8.1.1   Constructors

Let's start with the first method to be called in the life-cycle of an object, the constructor. Everything important about it has been said, but for routine use there are still a couple more questions which must be cleared up in order for us to be able to employ constructors consciously and correctly.

What, for example, does the constructor of a base class look like? How is a constructor called when you create an object of a derived class? We shall begin with the basic situation

```
class ClassX {};
class ClassY : public ClassX {};
```

In a call such as

```
ClassY y;
```

the constructor of `ClassX` is executed, followed by that of `ClassY`. In other words the object is built up in the same order as the floors of a house, with the base class as its cellar. Since we have defined no other constructors the compiler itself compiles a simple constructor for `ClassX` and `ClassY` each. This default constructor uses no parameters and does nothing. Its presence merely indicates that we have been able to create y.

A well-structured class usually has one or more attributes at its disposal. In order to initialize them we need more than a parameterless empty constructor. And so we shall define a constructor which fills a representative attribute aNumX of `ClassX` with a value.

```
class ClassX {
public:
  ClassX (int num) {
    aNumX = num;
  }
private:
  int aNumX;
};
```

What is puzzling is that the simple statement

```
ClassY y;  // Does not compile
```

can no longer be compiled. Why is this? As soon as we explicitly provide a constructor the default constructor is no longer created. The variant which we have provided needs an integer parameter, however, and so we have to somehow feed a parameter to the constructor of `ClassX`. The idea of doing this in the constructor of the derived `ClassY` is a sound one in theory. Nevertheless this and other attempts at definitions for `ClassY` fail.

```
class ClassY : public ClassX {
public:
  ClassY () {  // Does not compile
    ClassX (3);
  }
};
```

This is because the constructor of the derived class is not executed until after that of the base class. As before, however, the former cannot be called without parameters. There therefore has to be some prospect of calling the constructor of the base class with a parameter before the trunk of the derived constructor is reached. Where should this happen? It can take place only at a point in the code where the parameters of the derived constructor are available as variables, since these are typically used for the base class constructor. It must however take place before the trunk of the derived constructor is reached.

For this C++ prescribes the following notation. Initialization statements are added between the constructor's head and its trunk.

```
class ClassY : public ClassX {
public:
  ClassY () : ClassX (3) {
    ...
  }
};
```

The order of execution is the usual one: first the base class constructor is called with the parameters now in situ and then that of the derived class. This time the lines

```
ClassY y;   // OK
```

can be compiled.

Attributes of a class can also be allotted initial values in the initialization list. In order to test this procedure we supply the derived class with an attribute. In order to be able to control the values of the attributes of the two classes when an object is created, we define two parameters for the constructor. One is passed on to the base class, the other to its own attribute. The two initialization statements are separated by a comma.

```
class ClassY : public ClassX {
public:
  ClassY (int numX, int numY)
    : ClassX (numX), aNumY (numY) {
    ...
  }
private:
  int aNumY;
};
```

If we now want to create a ClassY object it will look like this:

```
ClassY y (2, 4);
```

> **Tip** In a constructor's initialization list attributes of the class can be initialized and the constructor of a direct base class called.

You may have just turned back to Part I to look up how on earth we were able to create an object of a derived class there without an initialization list. After all we did not call the constructor of `Pair` in the constructor of `Date`. The trick was to define two constructors for `Pair`, one with two parameters and one without parameters. The latter was implicitly used when a `Date` object was created.

Parameterless constructors are far from worthless. They make objects manageable and despite their simplicity of use make a controlled initialization possible. We would do well to attach a parameterless constructor to the class `text`. But its function must ensure that the pointer attribute of `Text` does not point in some arbitrary direction. The whole definition is as follows:

```
Text::Text () : aTextPtr (NULL) {}
```

We do not need to worry about the fact that a pointer with `NULL` value leads to errors in the other methods of `Text`. Both the `cout <<` in the method `output` and the `delete` in the destructor support `char*` with `NULL` value.

The basic constructor can be of assistance to us, for example, in a situation where we have to pass a `Text` object to a method which we do not want to supply with any text. The method might look like this:

```
output (int num, const Text& text) {
  cout << num;
  text.output ();
}
```

We can create dummy text to cover instances where we want to output the number only.

```
Text dummy;
output (1040, dummy);
```

Even simpler is to use a notation in which we do not even bother to name the object. It is created just for the method call and is removed again at the end of its block.

```
output (1040, Text ());
```

The constructor of a nameless object can if necessary be assigned parameters.

```
outputCopy (1040, Text (" in words one thousand and forty"));
```

If a class has a constructor with precisely one parameter, the constructor call can be written like an assignment. `Text` is such a class, and the next two calls are equivalents.

```
Text text1 = "Constructor with one parameter";
Text text2 ("Constructor with one parameter");
```

8.1.2 Destructors

The order in which destructors are executed is the exact opposite of that for constructors. First to be called is the destructor of the derived class, then that of the base class. A demolition firm deals with houses in a similar fashion.

The most important formal rule for writing a destructor is that it should always be defined as `virtual` if there is only a remote likelihood of using the class as a base class. Let's have a look at a simple derivation constellation. Both of the classes involved have a pointer attribute, the contents of which they free in the correct and proper manner in the destructor.

```
class ClassA {
public:
  ...
  ~ClassA () {
    delete[] aTextAPtr;
  }
private:
  char* aTextAPtr;  // Free pointer
}
class ClassB : public ClassA {
public:
  ...
  ~ClassB () {
    delete[] aTextBPtr;  // Free pointer
  }
private:
  char* aTextPtr;
};
```

When we manipulate dynamic `ClassB` objects we can point to them with a `ClassA` pointer. Derived objects are always passed according to type as base class objects.

```
ClassA* aPtr = new ClassB;
```

The freeing process is a bit of a headache however. In the line

```
delete aPtr; // Only ~ClassA executed
```

only the destructor of ClassA is called but not that of ClassB. It is impossible for the compiler to spot that the pointer is actually pointing to an object of the derived class, and therefore it calls only the destructor of the type it knows about. Consequently the text to which the pointer attribute of ClassB is pointing is not freed! There is a leak in the memory.

You can insure against such hidden gaps in your memory management by consistently declaring base class destructors as virtual.

```
class ClassA {
  ...
  virtual ~ClassA () {
    delete[] aTextAPtr;
  }
  ...
};
```

Warning You should always declare base class destructors as virtual, otherwise you run the risk of a memory leak.

The destructors of all derived classes are automatically virtual, and a call such as the following will find the right destructor.

```
ClassA* aPtr = new ClassB;
...
delete aPtr;  // ~ClassB is also executed
```

8.2 Methods with a special function

In the previous chapters we have dug deep in the object-oriented box of tricks. In doing so one of our initial aims, namely that self-defined objects are to be treated exactly like elementary variables, has been somewhat pushed into the background.

The Text class is a representative example of our efforts at implementation. It has a constructor and a destructor method. This makes the following statements possible:

```
{
  Text greeting ("Hello!"); // Call to constructor
} // Destructor is called
```

We have to pay for this however. The constructor acquires the same amount of memory as the length of the text passed to it and copies it into the area of memory allocated to it. The destructor frees the memory again.

But what is happening in the following lines?

```
Text name1 ("William");
Text name2 ("Harold");
name1 = name2;  // Is this a problem?
```

Here the value of name2 is assigned to the object name1. In int type routines the compiler makes sure that an operation like this works. For it to succeed with Text objects in the same way we have to define a special method which is called an assignment operator.

And what about this line?

```
Text name3 = name1;
```

This creates the Text object name3, and at the same time the value of name1 is copied to it. For this to happen the Text class has to be extended by a self-written copy constructor.

A comparison of the two Text objects

```
if (name3 == name2) { ... }
```

is not automatically as successful as one might expect. For this we need a relational operator.

In the following sections we describe exactly how these three methods are coded. We then explain what happens when the methods are not self-written.

8.2.1   The assignment operator

The assignment operator ensures that the value of an object can be assigned to another object. As far as the compiler is concerned the lines

```
name1 = name2;
```

and

```
name1.operator= (name2);
```

mean the same thing. The second variant features a method call named opera-tor=. The first variant is mostly preferred, however, because of its transparency.

You can define the assignment operator for a class yourself by writing a method named `operator=` which implements the assignment.

An attempt to write an assignment operator might look like this:

```
// First attempt
void Text::operator= (const Text& text) {
  aTextPtr = text.aTextPtr;
}
```

In order to make it plain that this method belongs to `Text` we have used the notation from the implementation file which recognizes the class name of a method. The parameter which is passed is a reference pointing to the text object which is to be copied. The fact that it is declared as a constant ensures that no change is made to the object to be copied. An assignment operator which modified the assigned object would be a cause for consternation. In the trunk of the method the pointer to the text of the object to be copied is assigned to the pointer to the text of its own object. This prompts two questions.

Who makes sure later that the memory originally allocated by the method's own object is freed once more? The object itself cannot do it since it no longer knows where this area of memory is. The `aTextPtr` attribute has in fact assumed a new value in the meantime.

Furthermore it is not clear to which object the memory belongs which both the method's own object and the object to be copied point to following the assignment. When the two objects try successively to free this memory again we have a problem. You are familiar with this situation from Chapter 3 on pointers in which we discussed the difference between flat and deep copies.

 In the second attempt we manage to circumvent both danger areas. First the memory originally occupied by the method's own object is freed, then sufficient memory is allocated to take the new text. Finally the area of memory to which the pointer of the other object points is copied into the method's own memory.

```
// Second attempt
void Text::operator= (const Text& text) {
  delete[] aTextPtr;
  aTextPtr = new char[strlen (text.aTextPtr) +1];
  strcpy (aTextPtr, text.aTextPtr);
}
```

We now have simple assignments functioning smoothly and without unwanted side effects. But there is a little bit of work to do before chains of assignments such as those in the next example are possible.

```
name1 = name2 = name3;
```

If we write out the assignment in full it will become clearer what is missing.

```
name1.operator= ( name2.operator= ( name3 ) );
```

The object `name2` has to use a return value when `operator=` is called which returns the new status of `name2`. For this purpose a pointer exists in each object called `this` which points to the object itself. You just have to de-reference it.

No sooner said than done:

```
// Third attempt
const Text& text::operator= (const Text& text) {
  delete[] aTextPtr;
  aTextPtr = new char[strlen (text.aTextPtr) +1];
  strcpy (aTextPtr, text.aTextPtr);
  return *this;
}
```

`operator=` now has the necessary return parameter. To stop it being modified uncontrollably from outside the parameter is declared as `const`.

The final extension to the assignment operator ensures that it also functions when `aTextPtr` is `NULL`. We have to provide this feature because the parameterless constructor creates a corresponding object. Furthermore we stop executing the operator as soon as we see that the object is assigned to itself. By doing this we avoid unnecessary logical mix-ups and still leave the object in the state intended.

```
// Final version
const Text& operator= (const Text& text) {
  // Begin self-assignment
  if (this == &text) {
    return *this;
  }
  // Normal assignment
  delete[] aTextPtr;
  if (text.aTextPtr != NULL) {
    aTextPtr = new char[strlen (text.aTextPtr) +1];
    strcpy (aTextPtr, text.aTextPtr);
  } else {
    // NULL assignment
    aTextPtr = NULL;
  }
  return *this;
}
```

The assignment operator is now complete.

Has it occurred to you that here we have a method of a `Text` object effortlessly accessing the private attribute of another `Text` object? This reminds us once again that private attributes are protected from alien classes but not from alien objects of the same class. We assume that objects know that they have to handle their fellow objects with care.

8.2.2 The copy constructor

The copy constructor does its duty in program lines such as

```
Text name1 = name2;
```

It creates a `Text` object and at the same time copies to it the value of another object of the same class. Being a constructor of the `Text` class the copy constructor bears the name `Text`. Its only parameter is a `const` reference to the object which is to be copied.

```
Text::Text (const Text& text)
  : aTextPtr (NULL)
{
  if (text.aTextPtr != NULL) {
    aTextPtr = new char[strlen (text.aTextPtr) +1];
    strcpy (aTextPtr, text.aTextPtr);
  }
}
```

In this case the errors from the first draft of the assignment operator have directly been avoided. The attribute is first initialized with NULL. Just in case the pointer of the object passed is not equal to NULL, new memory is acquired for the method's own object which subsequently receives a copy of the contents of the object passed. Unlike the assignment operator the copy operator does not require memory to be freed, since the object did not exist beforehand.

8.2.3 The relational operator

Finally we have the relational operator which is used when two `Text` objects are compared.

```
if (name1 == name2) { ... }
```

The fully notated form of the same condition is

```
if (name1.operator== (name2) )
{ ... }
```

A corresponding `operator==` method for the `Text` class uses a parameter of the type `Text`. In addition, however, it has to return a value which can be evaluated as the condition in an `if` statement, a `bool` value or an `int` value. Since neither the object passed nor the method's own object is modified by the comparison, the parameter and the method itself are declared as `const`.

```
bool operator== (const Text& text) const
{ ... }
```

The return value is generated from a comparison of the two objects. If we were to try to compare the attributes `aTextPtr` of the two objects, we should merely be testing whether both objects were pointing to the same area of memory. That hardly fits in with our idea of the comparison of two texts. What we really want is a comparison of the contents of the area of memory to which `aTextPtr` is pointing. This is easily accomplished with the help of the `strcmp` function.

```
// Relational operator, first version
bool Text::operator== (const Text& text) const {
  return (strcmp (aTextPtr, text.aTextPtr) == 0);
}
```

As previously, however, we must be prepared for the eventuality of a pointer attribute being a `NULL`. Two texts also appear identical when both pointers are empty.

```
// Relational operator, final version
bool Text::operator== (const Text& text) const {
  if (aTextPtr == NULL || text.aTextPtr == NULL) {
    return (aTextPtr == NULL && text.aTextPtr == NULL);
  }
  return (strcmp (aTextPtr, text.aTextPtr) == 0);
}
```

8.2.4 Default behavior

We have gone to some lengths to ensure that our text objects behave in every respect like simple variables. With hindsight it was irresponsible to define objects which were not blessed with all the useful operators. How would they have responded if we had assigned or compared them? Or in other words how does a class behave if you forget to implement one of its operators?

It is a matter of indifference to the compiler whether you implement all the operators that can be defined for a class. If you do not do it, the compiler will do it for itself. The default variants of the operators constitute a minimum solution.

When you define a class

```
class NoOperator {
public:
  int aNum;
  Text aText;
  char* aPtr;
};
```

the compiler automatically creates a copy constructor and an assignment operator. The constructor generated, as you know, will be parameterless.

> **Tip** The compiler automatically creates a copy constructor, an assignment operator and a parameterless constructor if you do not implement these methods yourself.

The copy constructor generated by the compiler simply calls the copy constructor of each of its attributes. You may never actually set eyes on this method, but it looks something like this:

```
NoOperator::NoOperator (const NoOperator& obj)
  : aNum (obj.aNum),
    aText (obj.aText),
    aPtr (obj.aPtr)
{
}
```

The automatically created copy constructor is really not such a bad thing. It is perfectly adequate for the attributes aNum and aText provided that the Text class has a proper copy constructor at its disposal.

The pointer attribute aPtr is the only element which is treated with less than adequate attention. The copy made of the pointer value is only a flat copy. This is exactly what a copy constructor is supposed to prevent. We cannot blame the compiler for not making a deep copy unaided. How is it to know how large is the area of memory to which aPtr is pointing? Is it text ending in a zero or a fixed-length array of characters?

Our conclusion from the experiment is that all classes which have pointer attributes at their disposal should define a copy constructor themselves. Default implementation is not sufficient. If we demand this for all the classes we use we can be certain that all attributes of a non-elementary type will provide an adequate copy constructor.

The automatically generated assignment operator also performs an attribute by attribute assignment, but this is not adequate for pointer attributes either.

> **Tip** All classes with pointer attributes should define a copy constructor and an assignment operator.

8.2.5   Preventing default implementation

Occasionally we find ourselves in a position where we should be well rid of certain methods. The assignment operator and the copy constructor are typical unwanted helpers since they are responsible for objects being duplicable.

For technical reasons, however, many objects cannot be duplicated. This applies to the termini of communications networks. If an object which constitutes such a terminus were duplicated, two subscribers would suddenly find themselves speaking into the same receiver with confusing results. A lot of objects generate administrative information in the constructor and destructor which would be corrupted if additional constructor and destructor calls were needed for a copy operation. Many objects are too large to be stored in memory twice, which is the prerequisite for the creation of a copy.

It is true that assignment operators and copy constructors are not the only options for copying an object, but they are so easy to call that it sometimes slips one's mind to do so. Copying an object element by element, on the other hand, is so tedious that you wonder about the sense of doing it at all.

But it's no good stopping the copying process from taking place by failing to provide an assignment operator. After all the Big Three default methods are generated automatically. The only way to prevent this happening is for you to define them yourself, making sure that they are not called. You therefore declare the methods in question as `private`. You can also omit to implement the assignment operator in order to exclude the possibility of an object being copied by an object of the same class.

If you implement the class `PlayingCard` as illustrated below you can be sure that no card in a card game will suddenly appear twice.

```
class PlayingCard {
public:
  PlayingCard (color color, type type);
  ...
private:
  operator= (const PlayingCard&);
  color aColor;
  type aType;
};
```

8.3 Overloaded methods

8.3.1   The basic principle

In Chapter 7 introducing inheritance we overrode the method `output` of the class `Pair` with a method of the same name in the derived `Date` class. At the same time we remarked that overriding works only if both methods have the same lists of arguments or, more accurately, if they possess the same signature.

In the last chapter `output` was declared as `virtual` so that the correct version of this method was always deleted when a program operated with pointers pointing to `Pair` objects. This too works only because all three `Pair` methods have identical argument lists.

What do parameters have to do with the clarity of methods?

A great deal in fact! First of all C++ lets you declare different methods with the same name provided that they are kept separate by their use of parameters. Secondly C++ searches for the correct variant of the method for you when you call it. This technique is called overloading.

Tip Overloaded methods are methods of the same name and of the same class which differ only in respect of their parameter lists.

Now you can see why we had to pay particular attention to parameter lists when we were discussing the overriding of virtual and non-virtual methods. Had we donated a parameter to the `output` method in its overridden form we would have been defining a completely different method. It would not have overridden the `output` method in the base class.

The following example makes the difference between overloading and overriding clear:

```
class Base {
public:
  void methodX ();
  void methodX (int num);  // Overloads methodX
};
class derived : public Base {
public:
  void methodX ();  // Overrides first methodX
};
```

Method overloading typically occurs in the same class. Two methods are defined with the same name but with a different parameter list. When one of the methods is called, the compiler recognizes from the parameters passed which of the methods is meant.

```
Base base;
base.methodX ();
base.methodX (3);  // Overloaded Method
```

Overridden methods are defined in different classes. They can therefore be differentiated according to the class from which they are called.

```
Base base;
base.methodX ();
Derived derived;
derived.methodX ();  // Overridden Method
```

8.3.2   When do parameter lists differ?

Since overloaded methods are kept separate by means of their parameters, these parameters must be sufficiently different. The problem arises when you overload methods with parameters which differ only in respect of a numerical type. C++ tries really hard to pass different numerical types together as one if the conversion is reasonably unambiguous. This often relieves us of some work, but unfortunately it is a case of the compiler being too kind for our own good.

Let us assume that you start with this class definition.

```
class Unambiguous {
public:
  void methodX (char character);
};
```

Then there is no problem about compiling and executing the following lines. In the case of both calls a method with a `char` argument is used. In the second an implicit conversion from `int` to `char` has to be performed..

```
Unambiguous unamb;
unamb.methodX ('x');
unamb.methodX (67);
```

However as soon as you extend the class by another method

```
void methodX (int num);
```

the same lines take on a different meaning. In the second call the variant with an `int` parameter is used without your having altered the code at this point. In its interpretation the compiler always prefers the option which requires the least conversions. If the two methods perform quite different actions you will find yourself spending some considerable time looking for the reason for the sudden change in behavior.

```
unamb.methodX ('x');   // char variant
unamb.methodX (67);    // int variant
```

The compiler's predilections are just as confusing if you go on to define a method with a `char*` argument.

```
void methodX (char* textPtr);
```

The last two of the next few calls will also encourage you to keep a sufficient distance between types of argument in overloading.

```
unamb.methodX (67);              // int variant
unamb.methodX ("Hello");         // char* variant
unamb.methodX (NULL);            // int variant!
char* characterPtr = NULL;
unamb.methodX (characterPtr);    // char* variant!
```

You can also overload methods with several parameters. You will ensure that overloaded methods differ in respect of the number, type and order of their parameters. The class `NParameter` produces a couple of variants of different methods of the same name. Only the last method cannot be compiled since the types of parameter do not differ from the preceding method. It does not help either that the parameter names are different.

```
class NParameter {
public:
  void methodY (const Text& text, int num);
  void methodY (int num, const Text& text);
  void methodY (int num, const Text& text, bool ok);
  void methodY (const Text& forename,
                const Text& surname);
  void methodY (const Text& surname,    // No good!
                const Text& forename);
};
```

We must be clear moreover that different return values are not a significant feature of overloading. In general return values do not have the same high profile as parameters. We easily weary of them and then simply leave them out. A method like

```
bool methodZ ();
```

can equally be called as

```
if (methodZ () ) { ... }
```

or even as

```
methodZ ();
```

Let us assume that you have made extensive use in your program of a class with method methodZ before deciding that the method is to be extended. And so you attempt to distinguish the overloaded version from the first version solely via a different return value.

```
Text methodZ ();
```

The compiler will not allow this. By making a declaration like this you have caused it to doubt what the methodZ calls in your program could possibly mean. Which variant of methodZ should be called if you ignore the return value when the call is made? As always in doubtful situations the compiler refuses to comply until you have declared yourself unambiguously. Its excuse is that you defined the same method before.

Tip Overloaded methods cannot be kept separate by means of their return values.

Despite the preceding examples you cannot accuse the compiler of not being thorough. It does a very good job of keeping apart as parameters a type, a pointer to this type and a reference to the type. Even the `const` property has the effect of distinguishing between two parameters in terms of overloading. The following methods can coexist without any difficulty.

```
class ConstPointerReference {
public:
  methodA (char);
  methodA (char&);
  methodA (char*);
  methodA (const char*);
};
```

We have taken the opportunity to examine a simplified notation which we had explained previously. Since parameter names do not help to make parameter lists more unambiguous you can omit them in the class definition. This is what has happened here. As soon as the method is implemented, i.e. in the `.cpp` file, the name of the parameter suddenly becomes important, since it is used in the body of the method as a variable.

```
ConstPointerReference::methodA (char& characterRef) {
  char temp = characterRef;
  . . .
}
```

You must tread very carefully when you are overloading methods in association with the `const` property because it is not always obvious how constant a variable is. If you are not sure which of the last two variants of `methodA` are called by the line below, try them out.

```
methodA ("const or not const?");
```

8.3.3 An example

If you decide to overload a method you should make sure that both variants mean the same thing. C++ makes no prescription at this point, but it is in line with our philosophy that methods with the same name do the same thing. Generally the need for an overloaded method in a program arises automatically when you find that a certain method should suppress other types of parameter, despite the fact that it should stand side by side with them.

Thus you might use a method `display` in a graphics program which displays a pixel. The parameters of the method are the x and y coordinates of the pixel.

```
void display (int valueX, int valueY) {
  // Display pixel
  ...
}
```

Later you find that you need a parallel method which displays pixels defined by polar coordinates, i.e. according to angle and distance from the center. Your definition is as follows:

```
void display (double angle, double distance) {
  // Display pixel
  ...
}
```

Now the name indicates that the methods do more or less the same thing. The code is written accordingly, and both methods do what has to be done to display a pixel. But if you decide to modify one of the methods, perhaps to display the pixel in color, you have to make sure that you make the same modification in the other method. Forgetful as we humans are, this procedure is error-prone.

For this reason you will very often find implementations of overloaded methods which end up by using a common basic method.

```
class Graphics {
public:
  void display (int valueX, int valueY) {
    displayInternal (valueX, valueY);
  }
  void display (double angle, double distance) {
    // Convert polar coordinates to cartesian
    int valueX = ...;
    int valueY = ...;
    displayInternal (valueX, valueY);
  };
private:
  void displayInternal (int valueX, int valueY) {
    // Now display pixel
  }
};
```

8.3.4　Overloaded constructors

You have already come across a special type of overloaded method without realizing it. The class `Pair` possesses both a parameterless constructor and one with two parameters. Both methods have the same name but different parameters in short, overloaded methods.

Overloaded constructors are particularly useful since they help us to divide the jungle of data out there into sensible portions and to work with code that has been tested. When you have had enough of passing the two coordinates which make up the pixel separately you can define a pixel class. You derive it from the class for number pairs. The new constructor simply calls that of the base class and passes its parameters on.

```
class Pixel : public Pair {
public:
 Pixel (int valueX, int valueY)
    : Pair (valueX, valueY) { }
  // Special methods for a Pixel
  . . .
};
```

You test the methods for pixels exhaustively until the `Pixel` class has become a practical tool which you can use. Later you will be able to add another constructor which receives polar coordinates. The conversion from polar to cartesian coordinates takes place in this constructor and the values are stored in the two integer attributes. You then get all the other methods of the `Pixel` class in the form of points in polar coordinates.

```
class Pixel : public Pair {
public:
  Pixel (double angle, double distance) {
    // Convert polar coordinates into cartesian coordinates
    int valueX = ...;
    int valueY = ...;
    // and store in attributes
    setNum1 (valueX);
    setNum2 (valueY);
  }
  // The rest as before
  . . .
};
```

You can now define pixels in any way you like and the compiler will recognize from the parameter types which of the two constructors to use.

```
Pixel point1 (210, 190);    // Cartesian coordinates
Pixel point2 (0.9, 50.0);   // Polar coordinates
```

It is even better if an overloaded constructor has only precisely one parameter. We can test this with our Text class, which indeed has one constructor with a char* parameter. If we pass a char* in a context in which we expect a Text object, the compiler implicitly calls the constructor, which creates a Text object from it. Let us assume that a method

```
void method (const Text& text);
```

exists. We can then call the method like this

```
char* textPtr = "Sahara";
method (textPtr);
```

or like this

```
method ("Sahara");
```

This saves us the trouble of creating a Text object ourselves each time we want to pass a text in quotation marks.

Tip Constructors with precisely one parameter perform implicit type conversion.

We have to accept, however, that there is a danger of the compiler using some existing constructor which we have never dreamt of employing. Let's assume that you have defined a class ClassA which is used by a method methodA of ClassX. In addition you have defined another class ClassB which methodA can do nothing with. For some reason ClassA has a constructor with ClassB parameters.

```
class ClassB {
};
class ClassA {
public:
  ClassA (ClassB b) {
    ...
  }
};
class ClassX {
public:
  methodA (ClassA a);
  ...
};
```

If you mistakenly use a `ClassB` object to call `methodA`, the compiler somewhat high-handedly performs a type conversion to `ClassA`. You cannot rely on the compiler notifying you of this error. The attributes of `ClassB` may not be at all sufficient to supply fully the attributes of a `ClassA` object with values. In this case `methodA` cannot be executed properly. But you will not notice this until the program is running and behaving incorrectly.

```
ClassB b;
ClassX x;
x.methodA (b);   // Compiles.
```

8.4 Operators

Many of our efforts to design classes do nothing to increase their effectiveness but do make them easier to use. Nevertheless our endeavors pay off one hundredfold if the classes are used a lot. Good manageable classes deliver well-structured code. You can then concentrate more on the problem you are trying to solve and you do not have to expend so much energy trying to get the better of the aids you need. Moreover well-structured code is less plagued with errors. Reason enough for a few more thoughts about the practicability of the classes we create.

8.4.1   An addition operator for texts

We now intend to expand the `Text` class in such a way that we are able to add texts. By adding texts we mean linking them together.

```
Text textA = "AAA";
Text textB = "BBB";
Text textC = textA + textB;   // Our aim "AAABBB"
```

If we think back to our initial experiments with `char*` this is a huge step. How are we to invest the + sign, which is actually defined only for numbers, with an additional meaning for `Text` objects?

The general mechanism for enabling us to do this is called overloading operators. By this we mean that we can supply virtually all the elementary operators such as +, -, *, / and also < and > and many more others with a special meaning for self-defined types. For this we have to define certain methods or functions which bear names like `operator+`. Perhaps you are having a double dose of déjà vu.

You are probably concluding from all this that internally C++ performs predefined functions such as + for numerical values and, at the same time, a function labeled `operator+`. These operators, which are unique to the language, use exclusively elementary types as parameters. If we wish to extend their scope to cover self-defined types we simply write an operator function which differs from the original operator function solely in respect of their parameter types. We have already examined in some detail in the previous section how the compiler's selection of the correct function depends on the type of argument. `operator+` is simply an overloaded function. The nice thing about overloaded operators is that they can be called so concisely and transparently.

This brings us to our second déjà vu. You are familiar with a special overloaded operator from Chapter 8, Section 8.2 on methods with a special function. The assignment operator functions in exactly the same way as the other operators. It just has the additional property of being automatically generated by the compiler. Moreover it is needed more often than all the other operators and is almost on a par with methods such as the constructor and the destructor.

> **Tip** You can make all elementary operators such as +, &&, > etc. significant for self-written classes by implementing the appropriate methods.

Before we shed light on the farthest corners of operator programming we should first solve the `Text+Text` problem.

First we add a new method

```
Text operator+ (const Text& rightAddend) const;
```

to our text class. Clearly it uses a `Text` parameter. After all we want to add together two texts, the second one of which is the object itself. We know from the chapter on references why the texts should be `const` references. We need the return value because we want to assign the result of the addition to a third `Text` object. Then the compiler makes sure that the line

```
Text textC = textA.operator+ (textB);
```

is executed when we write

```
Text textC = textA + textB;
```

The addition operator has to return a `Text` object. But we don't want to change the object `textA` on which the operator method depends. It would be a pity if an addition were to distort one of the addends. For this reason we have defined the whole method as `const`. As a consequence we are not able, as we were in the case of the assignment operator, to return the object itself as the result of the operation. Back then we used a reference to `*this` as the return value. Here by contrast we have to create a local object, fill it with the right contents and return it without a reference. It will cost us a copy operation, but it is all for a good cause.

Next we have the implementation of the addition operator as it may appear in the .cpp file. For a start we are assuming that the pointers of the objects in question are not NULL. To make the code a bit more transparent we are calling the parameter ra instead of rightAddend.

```
Text Text::operator+ (const Text& ra) const {
  Text ret;
  ret.aTextPtr = new char
    [strlen (aTextPtr) + strlen (ra.aTextPtr) +1];
  strcpy (ret.aTextPtr, aTextPtr);
  strcat (ret.aTextPtr, ra.aTextPtr);
  return ret;
}
```

We begin to implement operator+ by creating the local variable which is to be returned at the end. Then we acquire an area of memory large enough to take the whole of the text. We must make sure that strlen does not include the final zero byte in its count, but note that there must be room in the text as a whole for a zero byte. In other words the memory which we allocate for the linked texts needs to be as long as the sum of the individual lengths plus one byte.

The individual texts are then copied into the allocated memory. There is nothing special to worry about as far as the first text is concerned. When we copy the second text we have to find the exact place where the first text ends. This task is undertaken by the strcat function. It copies the second text on to the end of the first and deals with the zero bytes.

Now we have to return the pieced-together text object ret. The assignment operator ensures that it is copied correctly into a text variable such as TextC.

The case difference for NULL pointers makes its unwelcome presence felt again, safeguarding the operator for all contingencies. We use the assignment operator here too.

```
Text Text::operator+ (const Text& ra) const {
  Text ret;
  // Neither addend is empty
  if (aTextPtr!=NULL && ra.aTextPtr!=NULL) {
    ret.aTextPtr = new char
      [strlen(aTextPtr) + strlen(ra.aTextPtr) +1];
    strcpy (ret.aTextPtr, aTextPtr);
    strcat (ret.aTextPtr, ra.aTextPtr);
  // Right addend only is not empty
  } else if (ra.aTextPtr!=NULL) {
    ret = ra;
  // Left addend only is not empty
```

```
  } else if (aTextPtr != NULL) {
    ret = *this;
  }
  return ret;
}
```

That was a really fiddly piece of byte counting. At this point we become ple-
asantly aware of what we gain when we don't have to waste so much energy
every time we want to link a bit of text together. We just write the code out once
and use the + operator forever after.

8.4.2   A global addition operator

I can almost hear the protests from those of you who have a yen for aesthetic
programming, the intellectuals among you with a penchant for philosophical argument. Your objections are often helpful, though occasionally we simply have
to ignore them if we want to get anywhere. You point out that the function
operator+ has no particular entitlement to be a method of Text. After all it by-
passes the attributes of its own object and uses instead a local variable. Furthermore, you say, you have found an elegant alternative which at the same time sup-
ports type conversion. You have a bit of time to spare so suggest taking a look at
your alternative proposal.

```
Text operator+ (const Text& la, const Text& ra)
{
  Text ret;
  // Neither addend is empty
  if (la.aTextPtr!=NULL && ra.aTextPtr!=NULL) {
    ret.aTextPtr = new char
      [strlen(la.aTextPtr) + strlen(ra.aTextPtr) +1];
    strcpy (ret.aTextPtr, la.aTextPtr);
    strcat (ret.aTextPtr, ra.aTextPtr);
  // Right addend only is not empty
  } else if (ra.aTextPtr!=NULL) {
    ret = ra;
  // Left addend only is not empty
  } else if (la.aTextPtr != NULL) {
    ret = la;
  }
  return ret;
}
```

Yes, you are right, it is a global function. Global functions are bad news because they clutter up the available function namespace and their code is nowhere to be found. The idea of defining a global function named `test`, for example, is not a good one because somebody else may have the same idea, and then one of the two functions has to give way if you use the other person's code. The reason why things are a bit different in the case of global functions for operators is firstly because every programmer knows that these functions have a special significance. Secondly, global functions can be overloaded exactly like methods. Since you wrote the class `Text` yourself you can be pretty sure that nobody has defined an operator for it before. It is therefore all right to declare the operator as a global function.

Unlike your method of the same name the global operator has two parameters since it has no supporting object available as the left-hand addend. Moreover it is not defined as `const` since functions have no attributes which they could modify. Otherwise it does more or less the same as the method. The only problem of the function is its access to the private attribute of `Text`. If you do not want to forego the protection afforded by `private` you will have to turn `operator+` into a `friend` function of `Text`. This is done by making the appropriate amendments to the class definition of `Text`.

```
class Text {
    friend Text operator+ (const Text& , const Text& );
    ...
}
```

Which is better? The operator as a global function or the operator as the method of the `Text` object? Before you start assuming that we can define operators wherever we like, a word of warning. The two variants we have described are the only ones in which the compiler is able to deal with the useful shorthand form a+b. We cannot define `operator+` either in the right-hand addend or in the object which receives the return value of the addition. This highlights the merits of the global operator. It is particularly useful if we want to take advantage of implicit type conversions.

Tip Operators can be defined either as a global function or as a method of the operand's class.

Wherever we expect a `Text` object as a parameter we can also use a `char*`, since `Text` has a constructor with a `char*` argument. Provided of course that the pointer is pointing to a realistic collection of characters, the last of which is a zero byte. We turn this to advantage by writing the following addition using our method operator:

```
Text textC = textA + "BBB";
```

Since the right-hand addend is converted into the argument of the `operator+` method, the implicit type conversion takes effect, and two `Text` objects are linked together.

However the operator in method form cannot cope with the next expression.

```
Text textC = "AAA" + textB;
```

This is because `"AAA"` is not a `Text` object, and the `operator+` method is defined only for the left-hand addend of the type `Text`. Without an `operator+` method there is no method which might expect a `Text` parameter. Without the expected `Text` parameter there is no implicit conversion of `char*` into `Text`. This is not nice and is quite unfair to the left-hand addend. What's his neighbor got that he hasn't?

We are freed from this impasse by the operator in its guise as a function. It has two `Text` parameters and its effect on the two addends is symmetrical. If we write

```
Text textC = "AAA" + "BBB";
```

and the operator is defined as a function the compiler comes up with

```
Text textC = operator+ ("AAA", "BBB");
```

Next it engages the `char*`-constructor of `Text` and alters the line in

```
Text textC = operator+ (text ("AAA"), text ("BBB"));
```

Now the compiler just needs to execute the function and `"AAABBB"` will be stored in `textC`.

You must answer for yourself the question which of the two operator variants is the better. If you intend to use implicit type conversion often to generate a `Text` object automatically from `char*`, you can use a global function. On the other hand it is usually helpful to write code in which we can see what we are doing. Would you have had any idea before that the statement just discussed calls three constructors, three destructors, a global function, an assignment operator and a copy constructor? What if one of them has an error in it? It takes a moment or two to think where to look. We should not therefore begrudge the need to type in one or two characters in order to write `Text` when we mean `Text`. We are still left with the question of where we are supposed to look for the definition of a global opera-

TAKE THAT!

tor function in a large project. The class `Text` is located in `text.h` and `text.cpp`. If the operator is defined as a method of `Text` then we will find it likewise in these files. Global operators may be anywhere.

The skeptical tone adopted towards the operator concept which you can hear coming through this summary can be extended to all other self-defined operators. There are special fields such as mathematical libraries in which operators do invaluable service since they correspond exactly to our intuitive understanding of the subject matter. Matrix classes or classes for complex numbers cannot do without overloaded operators. But if ever you cannot say straight away what an operator is doing you should not define it. What is the point of an `operator&&` or an `operator%` where texts are concerned?

We shall now illustrate the other common properties of operators and extract a few more useful, concrete examples of operators which you might well use.

8.4.3   Other properties of operators

At the end of the book in the reference section you will find a list of all the operators which you can define yourself. If you want to override one of them for a self-defined class you should first check very carefully its meaning for elementary types. The self-defined meaning should as far as possible complement the central concept of the elementary definition. This is because it is not only the call code which is transferred from the elementary to the self-defined operator, but also the rules for evaluating merged expressions.

When you write `a+b+c` the order of evaluation is `(a+b)+c`. When you write the assignment `a=b=c` on the other hand , `a=(b=c)` is executed. This is of help only if the overloaded operators have the same order of significance.

Operators can be divided into one-digit, two-digit and three-digit variants. Many use return values, others modify only the object to which they belong. You can find out the type to which a specific operator belongs from its elementary meaning. The definition of a two-digit operator `x` of a class `k` which returns a value has typically the following form if it is defined globally,

```
k operatorX (const k&, const k&) {...}
```

or this form if implemented as a method

```
k k::operatorX (const k&) {...}
```

One-digit operators `y` with a return value such as the minus sign come in the following two variants.

```
k operatorY (const k&) {...}
k k::operatorY () {...}
```

However you will also come across operators which differ from this pattern. One such is the index operator `[]` which always expects an integer as the first argument. In the next section we define it for the `Text` class to give you some more experience of using operators, and also offer an implementation of the relational operators `<` and `>`. Finally we shall have a look at an operator which makes it possible to convert `Text` objects into strings.

8.4.4 A sideways look at operators `<`

`operator[]` is often used to access part of a larger object via an index . If you were defining a class `List` for concatenated lists you could for example access the fifth element in the list via `List[4]`, thus bringing the index operator into play. The similarity to accessing the elements of an array makes the meaning of the expression clear even to someone coming across it for the first time. For the `Text` class we can define an index operator which returns the nth character of a text.

For this we first write an auxiliary method which correctly returns the length of a text object even when its pointer is `NULL`. It's a useful aid in any case.

```
int Text::getLength () const {
    if (aTextPtr == NULL) {
        return 0;
    }
    return strlen (aTextPtr);
}
```

Now we can implement the index operator in the following manner:

```
char Text::operator[] (int index) const {
  if (0 <= index && index < getLength ()) {
    return aTextPtr[index];
  }
  else {
    return '\0';
  }
}
```

In the definition of `operator[]` we make use of the fact that strings of the type `char*` are at the same time arrays of characters. Therefore we need only map the indexed access to the `Text` object on an indexed access to the string held by the `Text` object. We have to be careful however that the user does not access an index which has no corresponding character. This includes minus indices and indices greater than the text length. The whole logic of our text class depends on the text itself not containing any zero bytes. The constructor cuts off the text passed to it at the first zero byte. This is why we are able to use the zero byte as a return value when accessing a non-existent character. This special significance of the zero byte should definitely be included in the notes to the .h file.

```
class Text {
  ...
  // Returns the indexed character
  // or the zero byte if the index
  // points outside the text.
  char operator[] (int index);
};
```

Without batting an eyelid we have defined the index operator as a method of the text class. By doing so we forego the option of an implicit type conversion when a call is made. This conversion is not very useful, however, due to its syntactic proximity to char*. You can write an indexed access to a text class as follows:

```
Text town ("Lincoln");
if (town [3] != '\0') {
  cout << town [3] << endl;
}
```

There is no chance of your formulating an indexed access with implicit type conversion since the [] operator is already defined for char*. The following example copes quite well without our text class.

```
char* townPtr = "Memphis";
char c = townPtr[3];
```

You would not have been able to define the index operator as a global function just like that with the same code. In fact we had to access the private attribute aTextPtr. This is not visible to a function which does not belong to the class, unless it is a friend function.

The last operator which there seems some point in employing for our text is the relational operator, which can be very useful when we want to put texts into alphabetical order. Since we also want to compare text objects with char* strings we shall define the relational operator as a global function. Text is sorted in front of other text when the first character which differs from the other text comes earlier in the alphabet. If two texts differ in length only the shorter has priority.

```
bool operator< (const Text& text1, const Text& text2) {
  int minLength = 0;
  bool text1Shorter;  // Text1 shorter than text2?
  if (text1.getLength () < text2.getLength ()) {
    minLength = text1.getLength ();
    text1Shorter = true;
  }
```

```
  else {
    minLength = text2.getLength ();
    text1Shorter = false;
  }
  // Compare by letter
  for (int index=0; index < minLength; index++) {
    // First different character found
    if (text1[index] != text2[index]) {
      return (text1[index] < text2[index]);
    }
  }
  // Otherwise decision based on length
  return text1Shorter;
}
```

Our relational operator relies wholly on the elementary relational operator of characters which, for example, sorts X before x and orders special characters, figures and symbols in a relatively arbitrary manner. This is routine in some respects, but you can easily modify the relational operator with a couple of case differences so that it meets all your requirements.

We can now conveniently compare texts with each other or with char* strings.

```
Text word1 ("Marjoram");
if ("Marionette" < word1) {
  ...
}
```

Cast your mind back to what we have done to get to this point. We first of all wrote an index operator as a method of the Text class which as such has access to the private text attribute. But this has the disadvantage that it can be used only for Text objects and not for char*. Then we implemented the Less-than operator as a global function. This causes an implicit type conversion if you try to compare Text objects with char* strings. Within operator< meanwhile we can be sure that we have two Text object on our hands. Since Text makes available the access methods operator[] and getLength we end up with all the information we need without having to declare the operator as friend of Text.

Such sleight of hand is common in the world of operators. This example is not being peddled to you as the golden solution for a relational function. The intention is only to give you an idea of how we decide on certain implementations of operator.

To be consistent you should define operator> when you have defined operator<. To avoid establishing two different sort orders you should use operator< to help you write operator>.

```
bool operator> (const Text& text1, const Text& text2) {
  return text2 < text1;
}
```

The equals operator should be compatible with the two inequality operators. If text1 is not smaller than text2 and text2 is not smaller than text1, then calling the operator= of text1 and text2 should return true. The same applies to the operators >= and <=. In the case of numerical classes the same care has to be exercised in order to keep operator+, operator+= and operator++ on a tight rein. A half-hearted decision for operators is generally a bad decision.

8.4.5   Type conversion operators

Type conversion operators are a completely different kind of operator than those discussed which invest an elementary symbol such as + with a significance for self-defined classes. A type conversion operator does what cast does for elementary types. You can see this clearly when a type conversion is written down in its rarely seen C++ notation.

```
char* string = char* (xPtr);   // Cast for char*
```

This notation exactly imitates the conversion operator. A conversion operator from Text to const char* can be defined as follows:

```
Text::operator const char*() const {
  return aTextPtr;
}
```

As a method of the text class it bears the name operator const char*(). Surprisingly enough no return value is declared for the conversion operator even though a value is returned by the method. This is explained by the fact that the type of return value is already defined by its name in the case of the conversion operator. The operator simply returns the private pointer attribute of the Text object. To stop a user of the operator being tempted to modify this object we have defined an operator for conversion to const char* only, and not for instance to char*.

You can use the new operator both explicitly and implicitly.

```
Text country ("Kyrgyzstan");
const char* aPtr =
  (const char*) (country); // Explicit conversion, C++ style
const char* bPtr =
  (const char*) country;    // Explicit conversion, C-style
const char* cPtr = country; // Implicit conversion
```

> **Tip** You can define special operators which perform conversion between two types.

The effect of such type conversions via self-written operators is very similar to that of constructors with a single parameter. Both are user-defined and convert from one type to the other. To do adequate justice to the relationship between the two techniques Chapter 10, Section 10.4.3 is devoted to them.

By now you will be used to the fact that all kinds of symbols can signify a function call, and so you will not be surprised to learn that our old friend

```
cout << "AAA" << 99 << endl;
```

is realized by an `<<operator`. It is overloaded for different types of parameter and is therefore capable of outputting both a `char*` and an integer. Chapter 13, Section 13.3 describes how to define an `<<operator` for self-written classes. But we no longer need this for our `Text` class since we have just made available the operator which performs the conversion to `const char*`. The global operator `<<` from `<iostream.h>` is on safer ground with this type. We can now output text as in the example which follows. The method `output` is now redundant.

```
Text text ("Operator test");
cout << Text << endl;
```

Odder still is the notion that keywords such as `new` and `delete` also function as operators and can be overloaded by you. We thus have the option of writing our own memory management system.

As you will now realize, operator programming enables us to redefine a large part of the language and holds out the tempting prospect of nights spent experimenting with the most audacious constructs.

8.5 Default parameters

The method `draw` of a graphical class employs two parameters. The first parameter describes the line to be drawn and has the same name. The second parameter is a truth value which defines whether the line is to be visible.

```
void draw (const line& ln, bool visible);
```

In most cases you will set the second parameter to `true` since the main purpose of a drawn line is to be visible. But in exceptional cases you would set the visibility parameter to `false` in order to delete a line which has already been drawn.

To avoid having to type in the value `true` unnecessarily often C++ offers you a simplified notation. You can give a default value for any method parameters. This value is simply written with an equals sign after the parameter's name in the method head.

```
void draw (const line& ln,
           bool visible = true);
```

You can call the method so defined either via

```
draw (ln1);
```

or

```
draw (ln2, false);
```

Although you can call the method with two different parameter numbers, you have to write them once. Of course there is still a third variant open to you, namely

```
draw (ln2, true);
```

But there is no difference between this variant and the first one. It is nevertheless useful since you do not have to alter your old code if you subsequently give a normal parameter a default value.

It happens just as frequently that in retrospect you might want to add a parameter to a method which gives it an extended meaning. This parameter can also be given a default value. In this case you do not have to adapt the rest of the code which uses the method in question in its original meaning. The method does not reveal its extended function until the new parameter is explicitly identified when called.

Tip Method parameters can be given default values which are located in the method head.

A few remarks in passing will help you to understand how the compiler deals with methods which have several default parameters. We shall define a method with two default parameters.

```
void method (int num1 = 0, int num2 = 0);
```

When we call the method with two parameters or none at all its meaning is clear.

```
method ();  // Equivalent to method (0,0);
method (3,4);
```

What does this next call mean though?

```
method (11);
```

Is the first parameter equal to 11 and the second parameter equal to 0 or vice-versa? In order to avoid such ambiguity the C++ standard stipulates that default parameters when called are replaced by the passed values beginning from the front. Thus the call is equivalent to

```
method (11,0);
```

Methods with parameters which are defined alternately with and without default values would be equal cause for consternation. For this reason the standard stipulates that the last parameters only of a method may be supplied with default values. Accordingly this declaration is correct:

```
void method (
  const Text& text1,
  int num = 0,
  const Text& text2 = "");
```

This one on the other hand is not:

```
void method (   // Does not compile!
  Text& text1,
  int num = 0,
  Text& text2 );
```

> **Tip** Only the last parameters of a method may possess default values.

8.6 Inline methods

We have used two notations for method definitions interchangeably up till now. The first directly inserted the definition of a method into the class definition if there was sufficient room for it. The .h file then contained

```
class Three {
public:
  int getValue () {
    return 3;
  }
};
```

If the method definition were so long that it might have obscured our view of the class definition we extracted it and declared only the method head in the class itself. The `.h` file then contained something like

```
class Three {
public:
  int getValue ();
};
```

The `.cpp` file contains the actual definition

```
int Three::getValue () {
  return 3;
}
```

In fact both notations mean the same. The first variant possibly executes faster than the second. In the first case the compiler has the chance to replace each call of getValue in the program directly by an optimized form. It would probably use the value 3 here. Whether it performs this optimization and to what extent it optimizes more complex methods is up to the compiler itself. The first notation just gives it the chance to optimize the call. As a rule this is worthwhile only for short methods. Often get methods, which return only the value of an attribute, are written in this form.

Since nobody likes writing code with side effects which are not directly observable, you can supply an optimizable method definition with the attachment inline. Then anybody who reads the program can see at a glance that the method is defined in the header file for reasons of efficiency. Unfortunately we then lose the clarity of the first notation since an explicit inline declaration is written in two parts.

```
class Three {
  int getValue ();
};
inline int Three::getValue () {
  return 3;
}
```

The advantages of speed achieved via inline methods are not sufficiently critical to warrant your rewriting all of your classes. As far as speeding up your programs is concerned you will reap the most benefit from some hard thinking about your algorithms. For this reason the real value of inline methods is that it gives you clear code. This is a supplementary benefit to the improvement in efficiency.

Tip Inline methods are short methods which are optimized during compilation.

A concept which is completely incompatible with `inline` declarations is that of the virtual method. As far as the compiler is concerned declaring a method as `virtual` means a double indirection which is not resolved until run time. First it has to find its way from the method name to the list of potential method trunks. Then it has to find the method trunk from all those available which belongs to the correct derived class. However, when it is given the job of finding a replacement during compilation, the multiplicity of combinations available sets the compiler off into a veritable orgy of substitution. It has to cater for just about every substitution option that exists. Your executable programs become huge and the speed advantage of the `inline` declaration is lost.

Advanced language elements

9.1 Exceptions

If you have had a particularly good programming day and have been working in a very concentrated way, it is unlikely that errors will have occurred. But even on good days like these, you might still have doubts about how to deal with exceptional situations occurring in your program. You naturally have to assume that all the other developers whose codes underpin the system have worked as carefully as you. This applies not least to the programmers of your operating system but to the engineers who developed the hardware and the electricity supplier whom you rely on to supply all the devices connected to your computer. If you have doubts about one of these factors, then you should try to anticipate unexpected occurrences. It is precisely these exceptional circumstances which can cause problems in complex programming. The simplest way of dealing with this eventuality is by detecting potential errors in the smallest components of your programs and either dealing with them straight away or reporting them in a conscientious manner. The exception concept in C++ has been developed for this purpose.

9.1.1   The basic principle

As soon as you are faced with an unexpected situation, you deny all responsibility in the hope that a more competent person will be able to deal with it for you. The variable in question can also be referred to as an exception, as it indicates that an exceptional situation has occurred.

```
if ( somethingStrange ) {
  throw int (13); // Error number 13
}
```

In order to take responsibility yourself, surround all the program objects in which exceptions could occur with a block as follows:

```
try {
  ...
  throw typeX (valueY);
  ...
}
catch (typeX& x) {
  // Deal with error here
}
```

The program flow will thus be interrupted in the throw line and resumed in the catch block. This allows you to enclose a faulty program object in brackets in the try block and deal with the error separately in the associated catch section. Both blocks will only occur in combination and in this sequence. The thrown type typeX may either be a basic type such as int or a self-defined category.

Tip The calling up of throw with any variable interrupts the normal program flow and sends it to a catch block corresponding to the type of variable.

9.1.2 Exceptions in methods

The performance and approach of the exception concept are determined by the fact that exceptions can be passed on externally through several levels of connected blocks, even from methods. Here is an example using a writeToFile method, which writes a text in a file. If the file does not exist, an exception is thrown.

```
void writeToFile
  (const Text& file, const Text& content)
{
  bool file exists = ...;
  // Verify whether file exists
  if (!file exists) {
    throw int (3);
  }
  // Write content to file here
  ...
}
```

In another method, in which `writeToFile` is used several times, the exception is caught and dealt with in a single `catch` block.

```
try {
  Text content ("It will rain at midday today.");
  Text file1 ("/usr/tmp/ file1.txt");
  Text file2 ("/usr/tmp/ file2.txt");
  Text file3 ("/usr/tmp/ file3.txt");
  writeToFile (file1, content);
  writeToFile (file2, content);
  writeToFile (file3, content);
}
catch (int error number) {
  if (error number == 3) {
    cerr << "File does not exist" << endl;
  }
  else {
    cerr << "Unknown error number" << endl;
  }
}
```

Here we have quite randomly used the output stream `cerr` instead of `cout` to show the error. Both output methods will become apparent to you when you call up the appropriate program from the command line. It is also possible, however, to separate the two data streams using specific operating system commands. The basic difference between `cout` and `cerr` is the fact that `cout` is intended for standard output, whereas `cerr` is only meant to issue error messages as in this case. It may be possible in an integrated development environment to redirect the two output methods to different windows.

9.1.3 Differentiating exceptions

A distinction is made between exception types so that you do not have to deal with all the errors together. You can thus define several successive exception blocks which deal selectively with a particular type of error. This means that within the same `try` block in a particular location a `int` exception is thrown, with a `Text` exception defined by us in another location. Depending on which program line is reached to throw the exception, the corresponding type-related `catch` block is executed. If several `catch` blocks correspond to a particular type of exception, only the first one will be executed. To prevent you from having to check all possible exception types explicitly, it is possible to add a non-standardized `catch` block. This is also referred to in the . . . parameter list.

```
try {
  ...
  throw int (1);
  ...
  throw Text ("Unexpected situation");
  ...
}
catch (int error) {
  cerr << "Error " << error << " occurred." << endl;
}
catch (const Text& error) {
  cerr << " Error " << error << " occurred." << endl;
}
catch (...) {
  cerr << "Unknown error type occurred." << endl;
}
```

It is possible to define several catch blocks for one try block. An exception is dealt with by the first catch block whose signature corresponds to its type.

Perhaps you are ready for a break now and want to read more later. What you should be doing is springing into action and sending a thank-you letter to the inventor of this fantastic concept. It is not too complicated, but just think how much work it will spare you!

If you want to write complex programs, you need to be able to deal with certain errors. The term program does not refer here to test programs, which produce the word "Hello" ten times. We are referring to railway control centers and packaging logistics systems, because these are the areas in which C++ is used. Your contribution to the system as a whole may be small but you should not call up unsafe methods under any circumstances.

```
void method3 () {
  method1 ();
  method2 ();
}
```

What if the hard drive is full? What if the main memory is saturated? Don't let these things worry you. In these cases you must take appropriate action and at the very least terminate the program in a controlled way. Without exceptions the necessary error treatment is extremely exaggerated for just a few calls.

```
int method3 () {
  int ret1 = method1 ();
  if (ret1 != 0) {
    return ret1;
```

```
  }
  int ret2 = method2 ();
  if (ret2 != 0) {
    return ret2;
  }
  return 0;
}
```

This type of code is found in C programs which do not allow for any exceptions. Error situations can only be transmitted in the form of return values. With exceptions we once again come close to the original scope of the code object. In addition the program remains transparent and the evaluation of errors is restricted to the `catch` block.

```
void method3 () {
  try {
    method1 ();
    method2 ();
  }
  catch (...) {
    // Error treatment
  }
}
```

An equally important aspect is the possibility of separating the implementation of error treatment. You can deal with errors once they have been sorted by type instead of by the place of their occurrence. The latter variant does not, however, do away with the need to differentiate between different error types.

Before we go on to examine error type in more detail, we need to consider the significance of the `catch` statement. It shows clear parallels with a method. For example different `catch` statements behave like overloaded methods which are executed independently from their argument type. The exception caught is transmitted to a method parameter in the `catch` block. It is governed by similar rules to those used for normal method parameters. You can and should at least catch them as a reference when dealing with complex objects in order to avoid replication.

```
catch (Text& error) {
  cerr << " Error " << error << " occurred." << endl;
}
```

You can also make use of inheritance features with exceptions, if they are logically related. It is possible to define a common basic category for all the exceptions thrown in a particular program. This can be linked up with other different exception classes with one or more special attributes which are necessary to describe the error in question – possibly the error number of an operating system call or a file name which cannot be opened. The example shown here uses a hierarchy of three exception classes.

```cpp
class Error {}; // Your general error class
class FileError : public Error {
public:
  FileError (const Text& fileName) {
    afileError = fileName;
  }
  const Text& getFileName () {
    return aFileName;
  }
private:
  Text aFileName;
};
class MemoryError : public Error {
  // Special characteristics of this error
};
```

In this way you can differentiate between error types very precisely and make use of their specific characteristics. No exceptions provide data which is unnecessary for describing them. You can also set the level of precision used to deal with errors without changing anything on the throw page. You can then start to deal with the errors on the basis of this block.

```cpp
catch (Error& exc) {
  cerr << "Sorry, my error." << endl;
}
catch (...) {
  cerr << "Unknown exception." << endl;
}
```

If it proves necessary to deal with the errors on a differentiated basis, you can replace them with the following codes.

```cpp
catch (FileError & exc) {
  cerr << " File error: " <<  exc. getFileName () << endl;
}
catch (MemoryError& exc) {
  cerr << "Insufficient main memory." << endl;
}
catch (Error& exc) {
  cerr << " Sorry, my error." << endl;
}
```

```
catch (...) {
  cerr << " Unknown exception." << endl;
}
```

In this case it is logical to catch the derived and therefore more specific error types before the general basic `Error` class. You should not under any circumstances neglect the exceptions which you do not intend to deal with specifically. You should take into account the fact that an exception which is not caught penetrates through all call levels from methods to the main program and thus terminates the program.

9.1.4   Using exceptions

It is not wrong to write an error text in `cerr` in the `catch` block, but this will not remove the error. A realistic way of dealing with errors is to take minimum reliable action simply to ensure that the program continues to operate. In general you will have the choice of avoiding the error or delegate the problem to someone else. Specific repairs are only useful and possible in very few cases. What is the point of making costly repairs if they are as unstable as the program itself? In the case of main memory errors, probably the best thing to is to terminate the program in a controlled manner. You should try to save what you can and then throw in the exception again in order to trigger the same response at the program level in question. It is possible to throw an exception that has just been caught again simply by `throw` with no argument.

```
catch (MemoryError & exc) {
  cerr << " Insufficient main memory." << endl;
  // Save unwritten files
  ...
  // Forward error
  throw;
}
```

If a `FileError` exception is identified, the reaction may be quite different. If your program has the task of opening a large number of files, it may not be quite so dramatic if one of them does not exist. In this case, the files are opened in sequence in the `files` field. Any file errors that may occur are caught and ignored. The loop remains intact in spite of this error. All other exceptions are overlooked, causing the loop to break, and the error has to be dealt with on the next highest level.

```
for (int i=0; i<numberOfFiles; i++) {
  try {
    open (files[i]);
    cout << "File " << i << " OK" << endl;
  }
  catch (FileError &) {}
}
```

From the way in which the `FileError` is caught, you can see that you are not forced to associate the exception with a variable as before exc if you are not concerned with its content. The exception type is sufficient to identify the appropriate `catch` block.

In the last example we have also taken into account the limits of those situations in which exceptions are used appropriately. Exceptions are intended to indicate actual errors and not simply to state "does not exist" when they are daily occurrences. A meaningful `File` class functions as follows:

```
if (file.exists ()) {
  file.open ();
}
```

and not thus:

```
try {
  file.open ();
}
catch ( ... ) {}
```

This is not only supported by the fact that programming according to the trial and error principle soon becomes uncontrollable, but also that exceptions in terms of scale are slower than normal return values. You are well aware of the type of constructor/destructor disaster that can occur if an object is transferred to a method. This is equally as valid for exceptions which are created and passed on to the `catch` block. If an exception is thrown, all the automatic variables in the surrounding block must also be released and the execution stack corrected section by section until the level responsible for the error is reached.

If an existing error can be repaired in a controlled manner, it is properly dealt with in a framework of `if` queries rather than in a `catch` block. There should not be any exceptions at present. If an exception does occur, you can either delegate or ignore it. And there is no harm in making a note of it.

Because throwing an exception interrupts the normal program flow, there is a danger that the interrupted, and therefore incompletely processed, program could be meaningless. The remaining non-executed lines are significant after all. It is therefore important to ensure that the code in the `catch` block continues the initiated program. This typically means that all the actions begun in the `try` block will have to be terminated in a controlled manner.

An example of an action that has to be completed is shown in the telephone conversation in the following code section. The method is associated with a class in which an `aLine` attribute is defined. An `aLine` allows access to a telephone line. The purpose of the code is to start a conversation with Mr. Smith. If somebody else unexpectedly answers the telephone, an exception will be thrown. This means that the last two lines of the `try` blocks will not pass and the conversation will not end. If the telephone conversation were not ended in the context of error handling, the call would continue indefinitely at your expense.

```
try {
  dial.aLine ("01234/5678901");
  Receiver receiver =
    aLine waitUntilSomebodyAnswers ();
  Receiver expectedReceiver ("Mr. Smith");
  if (receiver!= expectedReceiver) {
    throw Text ("Somebody else has answered");
  }
  aLine.conversation ();
  aLine.hang up ();
}
catch (Text& error text) {
  cerr << errorText << endl;
  aLine hang up (); // Important or it will be expensive
}
```

A similar situation often results in memory losses. An error occurring with a constructor cannot be passed on by a return value, because the constructor does not have a return value. A constructor should therefore throw an exception rather than other methods to attract attention. If the exception is thrown after the dynamic memory was requested, it is as good as lost. The procedure can be understood on the basis of the `KLeak` class.

```
class KLeak {
public:
  KLeak () : aTextPtr (NULL)
  {
    aTextPtr = new char[1000];
    throw int (123);
  }
  ~KLeak () {
    delete[] aTextPtr;
  }
```

```
private:
  char* aTextPtr;
};
```

If a KLeak is applied as an automatic variable, an exception is immediately thrown. The constructor can therefore not be completely executed. Automatic variables whose constructor calls have not been terminated will however not be included by C++ in the list of variables to be removed from a block. This means that, when the block is exited, the KLeak destructor will not be called up either. Consequently there is no point in releasing aTextPtr in this case.

```
{
  KLeak kl;   // Exception here
}  // Destructor will not be called up!
```

In order to solve the general problem posed by the KLeak, it is necessary to release the dynamic memories in the class in the catch block of constructors.

```
Kleak::KLeak () {
  try {
    aTextPtr = new char[1000];
    throw int (123);
  }
  catch (...) {
    delete[] aTextPtr;
  }
}
```

These remarks should not lead to the assumption that automatic variables will not be removed if the associated block is exited because of an exception. Automatic variables will also be eliminated if an exception occurs.

Error handling will not be dealt with in the same detail in the other chapters of this book as here. Such a degree of detail is essential for large, complex programs. For reasons of clarity, we will examine the different language elements separately, reducing them to their essential characteristics. These types of code examples are not intended to be exemplary in terms of failure safety.

9.2 Static attribute and methods

If you want to write a predator-prey simulation, you may define the Non-predatory fish and Shark classes, which are derived from the basic Fish class. Sharks eat non-predatory fish from time to time, but starve when there is insufficient prey. Non-predatory fish steadily increase in number, particularly when not many sharks are present. In order to record the number of fish remaining after each time interval, you require a superordinate calculation variable, which is altered automatically whenever the number of fish increases or decreases. The fact that this cannot be applied to attributes of individual fish is clear, as the latter can only be established by each fish. Moreover the calculation tool would be lost if the `Fish` object were to be removed. The procedure requires a global variable, with all the associated disadvantages.

9.2.1   The basic principle

There is a more sophisticated solution. From the point of view of content, the number of fish is a characteristic which should unquestionably be attributed to the `Fish` class. It is clearly an attribute of `Fish`, but it cannot be associated to each individual `Fish` on an exemplary basis. The `static` keyword, which can be associated with attributes, can be used to clarify this point. A `static` attribute does not belong to a single object, but to a whole class. This can be expressed as follows for the `Fish` class.

```
class Fish {
private:
   static int aNumber;
};
```

All fish share the `aNumber` attribute. If a fish changes `aNumber`, the new value for all the remaining fish can be seen. The calculation mechanism in the `Fish` constructor and destructor can thus be updated. If a `Fish` object is produced, the number increases and if one is removed, it is reduced.

```
class Fish {
public:
   Fish () {
      // Increase number in case of birth
      aNumber++;
   }
   static int getNumber () {
      return aNumber;
   }
   ~Fish () {
      // Decrease number in case of death
      aNumber --;
   }
private:
   static int aNumber;
};
```

The getNumber method to call up the attribute is also declared as static, because this also belongs to the whole class rather than to individual fish. It can be called up before the first Fish object has been produced. This means that it cannot be called up for a specific Fish object, but only for the Fish class. This is reflected in the way in which the getNumber call is written. It is obtained on the basis of the class name.

```
int number = Fish::getNumber ();
```

The question of setting the initial value for the calculation mechanism still remains. The compiler only allows for initialization in the implementation file fish.cpp together with the method definitions. This is because the value must be ascertained before the actual program is executed. It can however be called up before a Fish object has been produced and in this case is not cleared properly in the class definition. Initialization is carried out as follows:

```
int Fish::aNumber = 0;
```

Please note that you do not have to add static here, as an implementation file does not consider a class as a whole.

Tip Static attributes belong to the class as a whole and not to a single object. They therefore exist only once for the entire program and are called up for all class names.

Now that you have all the necessary components you can start playing the actual game.

```
cout << Fish::getNumber() << endl;   // issues 0
Fish carl;
cout << Fish::getNumber () << endl;   // issues 1
{
   Fish paul; Fish tom;
   cout << Fish::getNumber () << endl; // issues 3
} // paul and tom are destroyed here
cout << Fish::getNumber () << endl;   // issues 1
```

The values indicated in the comments corresponding to numbers are clearly only accurate if this is the first part of the program in which fish are generated.

The fact that a static method only belongs to a class and not to a particular object in this class creates a consequence. It does not grant access to non static attributes, because the latter always belong to a single object. The following class was not accepted by the compiler for this reason.

```
class Watch {
public:
  Watch (int seconds) : aSeconds (seconds) {;}
  static int getSeconds () {
    return aSeconds;  // Does not compile!
  }
private:
  int aSeconds;  // Non-static
};
```

This can be clarified by considering a possible use for this class. What value should be given in the first line if there are no objects in the Watch class whose attribute has been given? What value should be given in the last line? The one on my watch or the one on his?

```
cout << Watch::getSeconds () << endl; // Does not compile!
Watch myWatch (100023);
 Watch onHisWatch (432);
cout << Watch::getSeconds () << endl; // Does not compile!
```

> **Tip** Static methods should not use non-static class attributes.

On the other hand, it is quite possible to access a `static` attribute from a non-`static` method. This is always available and initialized. In this way it may even be possible to declare the `getNumber` of `Fish` class non `static` methods. To make the declaration

```
class Fish {
public:
  // Constructor and destructor as before
  ...
  // get number non-static
  int getNumber () {
    return aNumber;
  }
private:
  static int aNumber;
};
```

a `getNumber` from object names call-up occurs, because `getNumber` is a normal, non `static` method. It simply uses a `static` attribute.

```
Fish peter;
cout << peter.getNumber() << endl;
```

The result is that a call is not possible without an object.

9.2.2   References to static objects

In Chapter 6 on references we came up against a problem relating to return values. It is not possible to issue a reference from a method associated with an object that is only available within the method. Reference return values must always refer to an object that can be dissociated from the method call. In response to this requirement we have identified references to the attributes of an object as they are typically used by get methods.

```
const Text& getFirstName () {
    return aFirstName;
}
```

Another possibility is to issue references to static objects. This can be carried out in a CountryCode class dealing with codes for country names. Because the list of country names written out in full takes up a lot of space, it is declared in static form. This guarantees that it can only occur once in the program as a whole. The codeToCountry method, which transforms complete country codes into country names, issues an accurate reference to a list element.

```
class CountryCode {
public:
    static const Text& codeToCountry (int code) {
        if (code > 0 and code < 4) {
            return aCountries[code];
        }
        else {
            return aCountries [0];
        }
    }
private:
    static Text aCountries [4];
};
```

The .cpp file contains the initialization of the list.

```
Text CountryCode:: aCountries [4] =
 {"Unknown","Australia","Spain","Morocco"};
```

The transformation method could therefore be called up as follows:

```
cout << CountryCode:: codeToCountry (3) << endl;
```

A single copy of the country name to be issued is not given in this line!

9.3 Templates

9.3.1   Abstractions

Programming involves abstracting. Programming means recognizing the essential features involved in problem definition and developing a common solution. With the help of a few parameters, the abstract solution to an entire problem class can then be reconverted to a concrete solution for a specific problem.

The first abstraction step to be carried out in programming is that of constants to variables. A substitute figure is used and the calculations are made with this dummy instead of the fixed figure. When the program is executed the same step is carried out in reverse. The variable is replaced by a fixed figure. It is only at this stage that it becomes usable.

```
figure = 1;             // Variable realised as value
cout << figure << endl;  // Value is now usable
```

The next abstraction level consists of types. A type is a dummy for a particular variable, which in turn is a dummy for a specific value. Two definition steps have to be carried out in order to move from a type to a value. A variable of the type is defined and then a value is attributed to it.

```
int figure;  // Type realised as variable
figure = 3;  // Variable realised as value
cout << figure << endl;  // Value is now usable
```

We use a simple tool to help us to move forward in the abstraction process in a logical manner. We use the keyword `typedef`, which allows us to give a replacement name for a type. Here, for example, the name `FigureType` is given instead of `int`.

```
typedef int FigureType;
```

Using these methods we can easily deal with templates, the third level of abstraction. Templates can be described as higher or standard types. The literal meaning of the term is pattern. A good example is a template which defines a list whose element type is unknown. It is only when this element type is stated that a specific type, such as a list of integral numbers or texts, can be obtained from the higher types `list`. We have given the replacement name `ListWholeNumbers` for the type produced so that the first and second definition steps can be written down separately. A list of integral numbers could be generated and used as follows.

```
// Definition template to type
typedef list<int> IntList;
// Definition type to variable
 ListWholeNumbers myList;
// Definition variable to value
 myList.add (3);
...
// Value is now usable
cout << myList<< endl;
```

You should ensure that the miraculous generation of the type is not accounted for by the `typedef`. A `typedef` simply gives a succinct name for another type. It is the template system which allows for the generation of as many types as necessary from the `list` requiring only minimal instructions. Before we consider how a higher type such as a `list` is defined, we should make a distinction with the other type definitions which can be parameterized. A field definition of a constant length is given below for the previous example. We have also written this using `typedef` to allow for comparison.

```
typedef char CharacterField[4];
CharacterField myField;
myField [0] = 'a';
...
```

The `CharacterField` type has been redefined here too before declaring the `myField` variable and attributing a value to it. The difference, however, is that we have used the constant 4 in the field example to describe the `Character-Field` type to be defined. In the list example, we have used a type to describe the type to be defined. We have used a type as a parameter rather than as a variable or a simple constant. This has allowed us to specify the most important characteristic of the template.

Tip Templates are abstract definitions which become specific definitions when a type parameter is used.

Templates can be used both as classes and functions.

9.3.2   Classes as templates

Let us try out the process. Let us assume that we want to write a class for pairs of values similar to our Pair class. However, we may not want to determine the value type yet, or we may simply want to write the class and be able to use it for all types.

```
template <class T> class valuePair {
public:
  valuePair (const T& value1, const T& value2) {
    aValue1 = value1;
    aValue2 = value2;
  }
  const T& getValue1() {
    return aValue1;
  }
  const T& getValue2() {
    return aValue2;
  }
private:
  T aValue1;
  T aValue2;
};
```

This definition is not at all unusual. All the places where we would otherwise have entered a specific type are now marked by a T. We established the meaning of the dummy T in the first line. By adding template<class T> before the actual class definition, we indicate that this is the point where a class definition applying equally to all possible T types begins. In order to make this meta-class into a real one, we simply need to instantiate it as outlined in the list example.

```
typedef valuePair<int> FigurePair; // Pair of integral numbers
typedef valuePair<text> TextPair;  // Pair of text values
```

Since we now have access to genuine classes, we can use them to create and apply objects. The FigurePair class behaves in exactly the same way as if we had written the valuePair definitions and replaced all the Ts by ints.

```
FigurePair fp (14, 92);
cout << fp.getValue1 () << endl;
int figure = 3 + fp.getValue2 ();
```

The `TextPair` class, which has the same structure, can easily cope with text values.

```
TextPair tp ("Tom", "Thumb");
cout << tp.getValue2 () << endl;
Text text = tp.getValue () + "John";
```

> **Tip** Template classes are classes in whose definitions one or more types have been replaced by dummies. It is only when the type parameters are set that a template class becomes a real class.

The concept of instantiation has an additional meaning as far as templates are concerned. If you create a type from a template by using a specific type for the T parameter, you instantiate a template. The result of this instantiation is a class such as `TextPair`. This class can in turn be instantiated by normal language usage and obtains an object such as `tp`.

9.3.3 Possible traps

The advantages of templates over simple classes are obvious. However, great care needs to be taken when programming. If a class is implemented directly without deviating via a template, it is tested with regard to a few different parameters. You should check what happens when particularly large or particularly small values are transmitted to the methods. The effect of negative figures and empty strings should also be observed. You should call up the methods in different sequences and check whether their behavior corresponds to expectations.

The test procedure is more difficult with templates. A template cannot be tested directly, as it has to be made into a class by entering a specific type T. This can then be tested on the understanding that the cases to be tested will be considerably limited. A `list<int>` can operate smoothly whilst the corresponding `list<myType>` is having problems because of an error in the template definition. The template may require an assignment operator to be defined for the T type or the template may only operate for digital types, as it divides and multiplies T type objects.

Look at the next example. The `safe` template protects all types of variable against unauthorized use. It is only when the password is transmitted to the `output` method which was used to instantiate the safe that its content is divulged.

```
template<class T>  class Safe {
public:
  Safe (const T& obj, char* password) {
    aObj = obj;
    aPassword = new char [strlen (password) +1];
    strcpy (aPassword, password);
  }
  ~Safe () {
    delete[] aPassword;
  }
  void output (char* password) {
    if (0 == strcmp (password, aPassword)) {
      cout << aObj << endl;
    } else {
      cout << "Password incorrect." << endl;
    }
  }
private:
  char* aPassword;
  T aObj;
};
```

You can use a safe to protect texts in the following way. We have left out the in-termediate step involving a typedef. It is clear but not necessary.

```
Text message ("Secret");
Safe<Text> protected (message, "drowssaP");
```

When attempting to access

```
protected.output ("ABC");
```

```
Incorrect password.
```

is issued. Only second access with correct password

```
and protected output ("drowssaP");
```

issues

```
secrets
```

Perfect. This means that safe has not been sufficiently tested. If we use the template with another class, we soon come up against the first error. The second line

```
Date d(1,2,3);
Safe<Date> dSafe (d,"XXX");  // Does not compile!
dSafe.output ("sdlkj");
```

cannot be compilecompiled. This is because the object to be protected in the current `safe` implementation requires a constructor without parameters for it to be generated. This problem can be solved by shifting the allocation of the transmitted value from the constructor root to the initialization list.

```
template<class T>  class Safe {
public:
  // Constructor
  Safe (T obj, char* password) : aObj (obj) {
    aPassword = new char [strlen (password) +1];
    strcpy (aPassword, password);
  }
  ...
}
```

It is now no longer necessary to create a `Date` object without parameters. Instead the `Date` copy constructor is used to initialize the object. The compiler accepts the problematic line but remains in the subsequent one.

```
dSafe.output ("sdlkj");  // Does not compile!
```

This is because `Safe` tries to issue the object with `cout`. If a class possesses neither its own operator `<<` nor a conversion operator for a basic type, such as `Text` has, it cannot be issued in this way. We try to respond to this failure, because the purpose of a template cannot be to oblige us to adapt all our classes to its requirements.

This should not discourage us, however, as the problems faced are symptomatic of the use of templates and we can therefore learn from them. It is easy to place high demands on the classes which can be used as `T` template parameters if `T` is used in the same way as a basic type. You should consider very carefully which operators and constructors are required for each statement within a template definition. They should be kept to a minimum so that they can be reduced to the lowest common denominator for basic types. Assignment, comparison and generation without parameters offer a good compromise between comfortable template programming and the efforts required to implement `T` classes.

You should also examine the `T`s that you use to instantiate a template in detail at the outset. Available operators with insufficient definition pose a particular threat. An example of this is the `Date` copy constructor that we have just used. We did not define it ourselves, as it is a default variant provided by the compiler. If `Date` had possessed a pointer attribute, an abnormal end would have been pre-programmed.

9.3.4 Functions as templates

We can define function templates using similar methods to those used to define templates for entire classes. We leave the type open when defining the function so that all possible types can be included. We have already tested the example for the int type.

```
template<class T> void exchange (T& t1, T& t2) {
  T temp = t1;
  t1 = t2;
  t2 = temp;
}
```

As you can see, the keyword class in the template argument neither indicates that it refers to a class template nor that T a class conflicts with a basic type. Do not let this worry you. You simply need to get used to this syntactical feature.

> **Tip** Template functions are functions in whose definitions one or more types have been replaced by dummies. A template function only becomes a real function when the type parameters have been entered.

When we call up exchange we enter the type in angle brackets after the function name. However, if the type is clearly defined by the choice of parameters, we do not need to enter the type.

```
Text text1 ("Radiohead");
Text text2 ("Eminem");
exchange<Text> (text1, text2); // Explicit type declaration
exchange (text1, text2);       // Implicit type recognition
```

9.3.5 Templates or interface inheritance?

The next example shows the limits within which templates can be profitably used. The template function average averages three values for a given type.

```
template<class T> T average
   (const T& t1, const T& t2, const T& t3)
{
  return (t1 + t2 + t3) / 3;
}
```

Clearly the call only works if the addition and division operator has been defined for the type used. The latter must be consistent with integral numbers. A computer error occurs if we call up the function with text objects.

```
Text Huey ("Huey");
Text Luey ("Luey");
Text Duey ("Duey");
Text theDucks =
  average (Huey, Luey, Duey);   // Does not compile
```

We simply expected too much of the T type. We could not state anywhere in the template function that T had to carry out addition and division. The task of averaging values is not general enough to be carried out by a template. This allows us to draw comparisons with another very different programming technique which, at first sight, does not appear to have much to do with templates. We are referring here to abstract base classes.

Let us assume that we want to write an average function, whose parameter list clearly implies that it must be possible to add and divide the objects to be averaged. We can do this by defining an abstract base class, which specifies the required operations as purely virtual methods.

```
class Indirect {
public:
  // Division with integral number
  virtual Indirect operator/ (int) const = 0;
  // Addition
  virtual Indirect operator+
    (const Indirect& m) const = 0;
};
```

If we want to write the average function as a normal function with Averageable parameters, we can be sure that addition and division will be possible.

```
Indirect abstrAverage (const Indirect& m1,
  const Indirect& m2, const Indirect& m3)
{
  return (m1 + m2 + m3) / 3;
}
```

The solution is not perfect, which is why it highlights the advantages and disadvantages of both programming techniques. How, for example, could a user make use of the abstrAverage function? Only by deriving his required classes from Indirect and defining purely virtual methods.

```
class Temperature : public Indirect {
public:
  virtual Indirect operator/ (int) const {
    ...
  }
```

```
virtual Indirect operator+ (const Indirect& m) const {
    ...
}
// Additional methods
...
}
```

The user can now average temperature values.

```
Temperature morning (11);
Temperature midday (23);
Temperature evening (16);
Temperature daytime_average  =
 abstrAverage (morning, midday, evening);
```

But at what cost! We are dealing with a powerful temperature class, which probably also masters transformations from Celsius to Kelvin and Fahrenheit and much more besides. We are transcribing it so that it can be used for brief abstr-Average functions. This was not necessary with the template solution. In that case, we were able to use any T type. As long as it mastered addition and division, it could be used for average.

With the abstract base class solution, we oblige all users to change their classes in such as way that they inherit our base class. At the same time, we deny all basic types access to our function. The double type masters addition and division better than most, but it does not derive from Indirect and we cannot do anything to make it so. This means that we cannot us it as a parameter for averageAbstr.

The lack of type security within the Indirect derivative tree is also disconcerting. This can be seen as soon as we derive another class from Indirect whose task is completely different from Temperature.

```
class SchoolMarks: public Indirect {
    ...
};
```

We can now average school notes with temperatures without the compiler implying that our task is unreasonable.

```
SchoolMark firstSchoolWork (3);
SchoolMark secondSchoolWork (2);
SchoolMark averageMarks = abstrAverage
  (firstSchoolWork, secondSchoolWork, midday);
```

This confusion could have been avoided if we had called up the `average` template function. Because the `Temperature` and `SchoolMarks` argument types are different, the compiler cannot recognize on its own which version of `indirect` is intended. We are forced to indicate the types explicitly and in this way we attain the security required. The following function call cannot be compiled, which saves us a great deal of trouble.

```
// Does not compile
school marks averageMarks = average< school marks >
   (firstSchoolWork, secondSchoolWork, midday);
```

Using a function we have brought together a number of experiences with interface inheritance and template programming techniques. The function served simply as a useful example, as we could have made the same observations in a similar way with a different class. Neither programming technique proved superior as a result of the comparison, as they are used for different applications. If you want to write classes and functions that deal with a number of different argument types, including basic ones, without changing the types, templates are the best solution. However, apart from the standard operators, you should not place any further demands on the classes to be used. If you want to write more specific classes and functions, which can nevertheless be used for different argument types, then you should define an abstract base class which establishes the common features of these argument types. The user is still obliged to derive his classes from the interface in this case.

In addition to the interface inheritance solution, there is another programming technique which competes with templates. Macros provide a means of making almost any code object parameterizable. In contrast to templates, whose interpretation is strictly observed by the compiler, macros simply describe a text replacement which is carried out by the compiler procedure itself. As a result they are also unstable and prone to errors. The fiendish macro tool will be dealt with in a separate section (see Chapter 10, Section 10.2).

The potential uses for templates have not yet been described in detail. They can, for example, give a default value for type parameters which is similar to the default values for normal function parameters They can write template functions which operate with type parameters as well as type parameters. They can combine inheritance and templates. So before we examine the field in depth, we should emphasize a need for pragmatism.

Templates are powerful tools. However, appropriate care needs to be taken when they are created and relevant tests carried out. Many debuggers do not allow you to jump through templates from line to line, which makes fault diagnosis more difficult. Furthermore the compiler warnings, which you are supposed to be able to support with templates during programming, are often extremely unclear. You should only attempt template programming if you intend to instantiate the template with a sufficient number of different types. And even then you should consider whether you really want to write the template yourself. Perhaps someone else has already done it for you. Refer to the existing libraries, the most general one is the Standard Template Library (STL), which will be dealt with in Chapter 13. You will be surprised at what has already been tested and is available for you. With the insight provided in this chapter, you should not have any problem using the STL as you have been made aware of the possible pitfalls.

Hand tools

As well as embodying great concepts, which sometimes blur the boundaries between tools and theories, a language must also provide the means for carrying out simple tasks. These means offer no-frills assistance with everyday programming tasks. Some of them are extremely useful, whilst others are only worth mentioning because they recognize different codes used with these methods.

The section on type conversions is of particular significance, given that we have already briefly referred to most of them. We shall now examine them in context and consider when and how they can best be implemented.

10.1 switch and enum

10.1.1   A class example

Case differentiations are generally made with the help of the `if` instruction. If you want to branch the program flow using a variable which accepts a large number of alternative values, `if` proves rather awkward and unclear. Let us consider a `File` class which allows file access and records the status of the file as a whole-number attribute.

```
class File {
public:
  ...
  void open ();
  void read ();
  const Text& getContent ();
  void setContent (const Text& content);
  void write ();
  void close ();
private:
  int aStatus;
```

```
  Text aName;      // File name
  Text aContent;   // File content
};
```

The possible statuses given by aStatus are closed (0), open (1), read (2) and amended (3). Using the open, read methods etc., one status class can be converted into another. This involves carrying out the corresponding operations. To ensure that the necessary sequence is observed when calling up the methods, each method must check the initial status before it becomes active. The example below shows this procedure with getContent. Before the user can extract the content of a file, he must open and read it. If he forgets to do this, getContent will carry out this task for him. The status is then set as read.

```
//  getContent, first attempt
const Text& File::getContent () {
  if (aStatus == 0) {  // Closed
    open ();
    read ();
    aStatus = 2;       // Read
  }
  if (aStatus == 1) {  // Open
    read ();
    aStatus = 2;       // Read
  }
  return aContent;
}
```

Using aStatus, getContent checks which methods need to be implemented before the file content can be presented. We are working on the assumption that read will enter a value in the aContent attribute.

It is unfortunate that the two if blocks do not mutually exclude one another. You must ensure that the status is set in such a way that it prevents both from passing. There is no telling how open or read might change them. Alternative solutions can be obtained by bringing else into play. Unfortunately this often results in complicated nesting, which becomes even more complex as the number of cases increases, as shown below:

```
if (aStatus == 0) {     // Closed
  open ();
  read ();
} else {
  if (aStatus == 1) {  // Open
    read ();
  }
```

```
}
aStatus = 2;              // Read
```

10.1.2 Multiple branches created by switch

A possible solution is offered by the `switch` instruction, which can deal with
any number of alternatives in parallel. A whole-number variable, which is used
to branch the program flow, is entered in the parentheses after the keyword. The
different cases are introduced with `case` and concluded with `break`. If the variable does not accept any of the `case` values, the program run will continue after
the `switch` block.

```
switch (aStatus) {
  case 0:              // Closed
    open ();
    read ();
  break;
  case 1:              // Open
    read ();
  break;
}
aStatus = 2;              // Read
```

It is also possible to overlap the treatment of different cases. The `case` keyword
only indicates the point at which execution should begin. The flow can only be
terminated with `break`. This is exploited by the next `switch` instruction. Its
effect is identical to that of the previous `switch` instruction.

```
switch (aStatus) {
  case 0:              // Closed
    open ();           // No break!
  case 1:              // Open
    read ();
  break;
}
aStatus = 2;              // Read
```

If the file is open, it is read and the status is set at read. If it is still closed, it is first
opened. The following `case` does not stop the execution. The file is then read
again and the status is transcribed once more. In this way `switch` allows extremely precise, clear distinctions to be made between cases using whole-number
variables. You should, however, always bear in mind that forgetting a `break` after
a case has been dealt with and closed can produce very unexpected results and
it will be difficult to find.

10.1.3   Enum as a clear sets of values

Enumeration types, or enums, supplement `switch` perfectly. Enums are user-defined, limited whole-number value ranges. Or to put it another way, enums provide clear references for numerical values. Take a look for yourself.

```
enum Status {
  eClosed = 0,
  eOpen = 1,
  eRead = 2,
  eAmended = 3
};
```

This type of enum functions as a type. You can create `Status` type variables and attribute clear values to them.

```
Status myStatus = eRead;
```

This enables us to write the final code for the `getContent` methods.

```
switch (aStatus) {
  case eClosed:
    open ();
  case eOpen:
    read ();
  break;
}
aStatus = eRead;
return aContent;
```

Even though enums can easily be implicitly converted into integral numbers and back again, we should still define the status attribute as `Status` rather than `int`. We must then automatically consider the question of where the enum can be identified. Just as we are reluctant to define variables in a global manner without attributing them to classes, we also try to integrate enums into the name range of the class to which they most closely belong. How easy it would be then for two developers working at completely different ends of a large project to define enums with the obvious name `Status` which would only come into conflict in the case of joint compilation. Here the allocation is clear. `Status` belongs to `File`. The decisive sections of `File` are presented as follows:

```
class File {
public:
  enum Status {
    ...
  };
  ...
```

```
private:
  ...
  Status aStatus;
};
```

Whenever we use `Status` for other purposes than implementing `File`, we must indicate the associated class in scope style. This may be necessary, for example, if we want to call up the status in a `getStatus` method from an external source.

```
File logFile (...);
...
if (logFile.getStatus () == File::eRead)
{ ... }
```

When the `getStatus` method is declared, the enum type must also be fully qualified, because `getStatus` represents an interface which can be accessed from outside the class.

```
File::Status File::getStatus () {
  return aStatus;
}
```

Two further remarks should be made about the enum definition and the `switch` instruction. You should not allocate a numerical value to every enum value. If you do not do this, the numerical values will be allocated to the enum declarations from 0 upwards in sequence. In this example, the value names reflect the actual value of the numbers.

```
enum Numbers {
  eNull,
  eOneHundred = 100,
  eOneHundredAndOne
};
```

With `switch` we are still unable to deal with all cases which are not referred to explicitly with separate code elements. The `Default` case is provided for this purpose. The next `case` instruction could appear in the implementation of `write`.

```
switch (aStatus) {
  case eAmended:
    // Write
    ...
    break;
  case eRead:
    // Do nothing
```

```
      break;
    default:
      throw FileError (aFileName);
      break;
}
aStatus = eRead;
```

In the case of eRead we assume that the write procedure has already been carried out. We set the status at the end according to this value. Although we cannot do anything at this stage, we must specifically list the case to distinguish it from the error cases. The latter give rise to an exception in the default section.

The two language elements enum and switch do not necessarily belong together and they can be used separately. However, they complement each other so well that they are often found together.

Switch cannot be used if you need to formulate multiple alternatives which do not depend on a whole-number variable. If and else instructions are used instead in the following form. The decision variable in this case is a Text object.

```
Text name = ...
if (name == "John") {
  cout << "Hello John! " << endl;
} else if (name == "Mr. Smith") {
  cout << "Hello Mr. Smith! " << endl;
} else {
  cout << "Hello! " << endl;
}
```

The cases are mutually exclusive here too. Although this code is not quite as clear as a switch instruction, it at least avoids deeply nested blocks.

10.2 Macros

The fact that the most powerful language element of C++ is dealt with in a chapter concerned with the miscellaneous aspects of C++ requires an explanation. Macros form a simple language within a language. They can be used to establish instructions for text replacements in a code, which are executed before the compiler has seen the code. This has the advantage of providing almost unlimited freedom to make replacements and the disadvantage of subjecting the result of the replacement to a syntax test. Macros are therefore just as temperamental as they are powerful and we only recommend using them in certain circumstances.

10.2.1　A macro for debug outputs

Let us first consider the advantages of macros. A typical way of gaining insight into the functions of a comprehensive program is by creating debug outputs. The most important variable values are given at all the interesting code points. An impression of even complex sequences can be obtained on the basis of the output quantity. The output code for a variable known as `numerator3` might look like this:

```
cout << "XXXXXXX" << endl;
cout << " numerator3: "<< numerator3<< endl;
```

If you need to create a large number of outputs, writing the code several times is a laborious process. It is not possible, however, to write a method to simplify the process. The variables that may be issued can be of many different types, but when a method is declared you must decide on a particular parameter type. Only one macro remains in this case.

```
#define DEBUG(var) \
cout << "XXXXXXX" << endl; \
cout << #var" :    "<< var << endl;
```

You will see that the macro definition is introduced `#define`. All instructions beginning with a double cross will be evaluated by the preprocessor. This compiler assistant replaces your `include` instructions with the corresponding file content. It also helps to evaluate macros. The name of the macro is `DEBUG` and it possesses a `var` parameter.

We have simply integrated our code for debug outputs as the macro code and have replaced the special variable name `numerator3` with the general `var` parameter. The only element of particular note is the fact that we have replaced the original variable name in inverted commas by the expression `#var`. This is a particular way of expressing that the macro parameter is first evaluated and then placed in inverted commas. The following test, in which `DEBUG` is used, shows that the parameter is recognized as such.

```
double dollar rate = 0.7009;
char* magazine = "Time";
DEBUG(dollar rate)
DEBUG(magazine)
```

The outputs are

```
XXXXXXX
 dollar rate: 0.7009
XXXXXXX
 magazine: Time
```

The variable name was recognized by the macro and issued correctly! This is a little-known dimension of the parameter concept. As well as using variable values as parameters, we can also use variable names. As soon as we understand how the preprocessor works, the mystery loses some of its appeal. Because the preprocessor is brought into play before the compiler has compiled the code, the macros can be interpreted as a simple text conversion. Every time DEBUG appears in the program, it is replaced by its macro definition. The preprocessor nevertheless ensures that it enters the parameters given in the new code in place of the var character string. Because the replacements in your code are completed before the compiler appears with its in-depth understanding of variable types, the macro functions with character strings in exactly the same way as with numbers.

If you have managed to obtain an overview of a complex program flow with the help of the DEBUG macro and have eventually found the error you were looking for, you will want to discard the outputs. They would only confuse the end user of your program. You do not need to search the entire program for DEBUG in order to remove it. All you need to do is define DEBUG as empty.

```
#define DEBUG(var)
```

That is all you need to do. Once you have repeated the compiling procedure the outputs will have disappeared. If necessary you can reactivate them in the same way.

Tip Macros implement text replacements in the code before it has been compiled.

A number of details need to be taken into account when defining macros. Because the preprocessor is not as far-reaching as the compiler, macro programming requires more discipline from the point of view of syntax than pure C++ programming. The term #define must always be at the beginning of a line and must not be indented. There must not be any blank characters between # and define or between the name of the macro and the following parentheses. Line breaks within a macro definition must be indicated with a backlash \. There must be no further characters after the backslash. Blank characters after the backslash are particularly harmful because they are not in evidence but nevertheless pose problems in translation.

10.2.2   Risks and side effects

The actual problems arising in macro programming are not caused by inflexible syntax. The real danger is the fact that the effects of macro definition are not immediately obvious. If you make excessive use of the freedom offered by macros, one of the more rigorous compilers will soon bring you back down to earth. The best scenario is one in which the code produced by the preprocessor is untranslatable. In this case you may obtain extremely unclear error messages, but at least you know that an error has occurred, as in the case below.

```
#define DIFFERENCE(a,b) a-b
```

DIFFERENCE cannot be compiled with number arguments or with Text arguments.

```
DIFFERENCE(10,3);            // OK
Text name1 ("Tony");
Text name2 ("Paul");
DIFFERENCE(name1,name2);  // Does not compile
```

Error situations in which expanded macros create a code whose syntax is correct but whose content is inaccurate are more serious. An example of this is the outputting of a number via a pointer, the effects of which are most useful.

```
int* numPtr = ...;
...
if (numPtr!= NULL)
  DEBUG(*numPtr)
```

In order to check whether the pointer is actually engaged, you should first check NULL. For reasons of convenience, the programmer has used if in the variant without a self-contained block. This is permitted with one-line instructions. In spite of this cautionary measure, the program frequently crashes in the DEBUG instruction. What has gone wrong? By simply writing down what the preprocessor makes of the if instruction, the situation becomes clearer.

```
if (numPtr != NULL)
  cout << "XXXXXXXX" << endl;
cout << "*numPtr: "<< *numPtr << endl;
```

Now we can see straight away that if only applies to the first cout. The second critical line in which the pointer is dereferenced is always executed. This also explains the abnormal ends which occur with numPtr NULL. The problem can be dealt with by only using if with a block. The next instruction is as secure as you would expect.

```
if (numPtr!= NULL) {
  DEBUG(*numPtr)
}
```

This is one of the reasons why you should ideally only use `if` in this way. However, the macro itself can and should be placed in brackets in order to rule out unsafe applications.

```
#define DEBUG(var) { \
  cout << "XXXXXXXX" << endl; \
  cout << #var":    "<< var << endl; \
}
```

In this way you could solve this particular problem, but the general disguised effect of macros remains. Macro calls of arguments with increment operators are another good example of this. The helpful macro, with which the square of a number is created, is affected by this problem.

```
#define SQUARE(x) x*x
int i = 3;
cout << SQUARE(i++) << endl;
```

In this case, the square of 3 is not output and `i` incremented. Instead, 12 is output as the product of 3 and 4 and `i` has the value 5 at the end. This can be explained by considering the expanded form of the output line.

```
cout << i++*i++ << endl;
```

You can never be careful enough when dealing with macros. You should never push their application to its limits and use too many or too complex macros. A language which carries out rigorous syntactical tests protects us from more serious errors than syntactical ones and should not be seen as an unnecessary nuisance. You can easily put an end to the syntactical rigor of C++ using macros, but you will have to face the consequence.

10.2.3   Conditional translation with macros

Macros are often found in their simplest form, however, and can be used to advantage. They can be successfully used as flags to activate or deactivate different code areas. Additional assistance can be obtained from the preprocessor directives `#ifdef`, `#else` and `#endif`, which regulate conditional translation. In this way, programs can be implemented in specific variants for different operating systems without having to partition the code between different files.

Among other things, this general information class issues the operating system type as an enum.

```
class Generalinformation {
public:
  enum OS_Type {
    eUnix,
```

```
    eNT
  };
  OS_Type getOS () {
#ifdef OS_UNIX
    return eUnix;
#else
    returneNT;
#endif
  }
  ...
};
```

If a

```
#define OS_UNIX
```

appears in any part of the code before this class definition, the OS_UNIX macro is defined and the getBS method is compiled in such a way that it issues eUnix. If OS_UNIX is not defined, eNT is issued in all cases. This is clearly more benefi-cial if you want to write codes corresponding to different operating systems in a method. This is necessary, for example, if you have to develop and maintain the same program on several platforms. The code for software products which are used with a wide range of platforms appears with #ifdef.

It is clear that the inquiry with #ifdef does not execute the macro. #ifdef sim-ply checks whether a macro has been defined for the corresponding name. From this point of view, the lines

```
#define OS_UNIX
#define OS_UNIX YES
#define OS_UNIX XXX
```

are completely equivalent.

If #define and #ifdef are used for conditional compilation, there is a danger that the program could become confused. If there are too many alternatives to be dealt with, it is often difficult to maintain an overview of the code. It is there-fore important to take into account the omissions taken into account by the pre-processor in order to become fully aware of the code version to be compiled.

In some cases it is better, therefore, to write genuine if instructions in the code. This is only possible in method roots and not in situations in which a class defi-nition has to be partitioned into two different variants.

10

TAKE THAT!

10.3 Structs, namespaces, typedefs, unions

The language elements discussed in this section contain all type characteristics. Structs and unions have been maintained as categories of user-defined types since the language first came into being. We have already briefly referred to typedefs as alternative names for other types. Namespaces, on the other hand, are contemporary features. They prevent us from unnecessarily contaminating the global name spaces for variables. Let's consider an example.

10.3.1   Structs

There is often a temptation to define a class specifically when you simply want to bundle several variables with the same unit. Classes are quite wrongly viewed with caution for having to be written comprehensively. This is probably because it is possible to write any number of complicated classes. There is no reason, however, why classes consisting of only a few `public` attributes should not be written. If a class does not have any methods which use its attributes and require the latter to be consistent, the attributes do not necessarily have to be declared as `private`. An example of a useful minimalist class is given below.

```
class CAddress {
public:
   Text aName;
   Text aStreet;
   int aHouseNumber;
   Text aTown;
};
```

As all methods which use `CAddress` are clearly defined in other classes, their accuracy can be relied upon. Private attributes with public methods such as `getName` and `setName` would not alter this in any way. A slightly simpler way of writing the `CAddress` class is

```
struct SAddress {
   Text aName;
   Text aStreet;
   int aHouseNumber;
   Text aTown;
};
```

`SAddress` is a so-called struct, with exactly the same value as `CAddress`. Structs are classes whose attributes are of a publicly accessible nature. It is therefore no mistake that the `public` addition is missing from the `struct` definition. The meaning of structs is clearer, however, if we see it in terms of a class predecessor

TAKE THAT!

10

or an n-tuple. Copies of structs are created in the same way as copies of classes. The elements of a structs can also be accessed by the point operator.

```
SAddress myaddress;
myaddress.aName = "Joe";
```

A struct is a class whose default attributes are `public`.

The developers of C++ were so keen to provide successful data encapsulation that they did not simply introduce the keyword `class` that was not used in C to set private attributes as defaults. The C++ documentation also uses general classes and avoids structs. Therefore the latter are practically insignificant in C++. The only advantage of structs over classes is their compatibility with C. If you use a library written in C which requires structs as parameters, you should enter them.

10.3.2   Namespaces

Namespaces reduce the class concept to a different feature from the one highlighted by structs, namely the namespace. Namespaces are code areas within which all the defined types can be accessed by each other without an additional name in scope style. We have tested this with enums which belong to the namespace of a class. The enum `status` of the `File` class can only be used outside the class with class names. Both the type `Status` and specific values such as `eClosed` are fully qualified with `File::`.

```
File::Status myStatus = File::eClosed;
```

This extra effort is compensated for by the fact that an enum with the same name in another namespace does not collide with `Status` within `File`.

```
class NetworkConnection {
public:
  enum Status {
    ...
  };
  ...
};
```

Let us go back to the actual namespace itself. Using the keyword `namespace` you can mark a code area, which is simply a namespace, without possessing the other characteristics of a class such as default constructors and default operators. You can define types, variable and functions within a namespace.

```
namespace NameSpaceX {
  int number;
  void function () { ... }
  enum Status { ... };
  class ClassA { ... };
}
```

However in contrast to a class, a namespace is not instantiated in order to access its variables and functions.

```
NameSpaceX::number = 13;
NameSpaceX::function ();
NameSpaceX::Status status = NameSpaceX::eValue1;
NameSpaceX::ClassA a ("Star Wars");
a.output ();
```

The variables defined in the namespace tend to resemble the static attributes and methods of a class. Another difference between namespaces and classes is the possibility of defining namespaces by sections. The definition of NameSpaceX can be partitioned between two different files. One contains

```
namespace NameSpaceX {
  int number;
  void function () {;}
}
```

the other contains the rest.

```
namespace NameSpaceX {
  enum Status { ... };
  class ClassA { ... };
}
```

This means that the code can be divided into separate areas for different programmers or subject areas in a large program. Collisions and ambiguities are therefore more or less ruled out. The program section can nevertheless be accessed from anywhere with the corresponding additional name.

If a namespace frequently uses elements from another one, it can be inconvenient to use the latter's name as a qualification every time. The using directive alleviates this type of relationship between namespaces. It indicates which class of another namespace can be used in the original namespace without being qualified. Here we have used a namespace of `ClassA` from `NameSpaceX`.

```
namespace NameSpaceY {
  using NameSpaceX::ClassA;
  ClassA a;  // OK
  ...
}
```

As you can see, all the elements of another namespace can be used without a qualified addition. This can be noted as follows.

```
namespace NameSpaceZ {
  using namespace NameSpaceX;
  ClassA a;  // OK
  ...
}
```

It is in your interest to keep the `using` instructions as brief as possible in order to guarantee complete protection against the name collisions and ambiguities inherent in namespaces.

Even if this is not consistent with the examples in this book, the conception of C++ is such that any codes that you may write can be included in a namespace. A namespace is not in competition with other grouping language elements such as classes or structs. Instead it offers an unobtrusive addition to the latter. Namespaces can also be added to an existing project without too much trouble. The language planners explain how this is done using the standard library contained in the namespace `std` in Chapter 13.

10.3.3 Typedefs

A typedef can be used to give a variable type a replacement name. The purpose of this is twofold. Complicated types such as arrays or template types can be named more succinctly. In addition, by changing this kind of type definition in an entire program, it is possible to change the meaning of all the positions which use the alternative name.

A typedef is defined by the keyword followed by the type in question and the alternative name. They can then be used in the same way as any other type. This is an example of a typedef for the new Array5 type in action.

```
typedef double Array5[5];
Array5 myArray = {1.31, 1.02, 1.54, 3.10, 2.45};
```

Template instantiations are often combined with typedefs. Let us assume that `list` is a list template which uses an `insert` method.

```
typedef list<text> Book;
Book mobyDick;
Text page1 ("...");
mobyDick.insert (page1);
```

In spite of the two names, as far as the compiler is concerned, `mobyDick` is also a `list<Text>` type. `Book` and `list<Text>` are not considered as different types but as synonyms. A typedef is therefore considerably more reliable than a macro, which replaces the `Book` character string by the `list<Text>` character string. Typedefs are observed by the compiler and can naturally only be used in code positions in which the syntax provides for a variable type.

Typedefs give replacement names for types

As has already been pointed out, typedefs are useful if you suspect at the outset that type replacements will have to be made throughout the program. If, for example, you write a program which carries out mathematical calculations, you can work with the `decimalnumber` type.

```
typedef double decimalnumber;
```

All your methods will use this type as input and output parameters. If the calculation capacity proves to be insufficient, you can alter the typedef in the central position.

```
typedef long double decimalnumber;
```

After further translation, your program will operate more accurately without any more alterations being required. Assuming of course that your methods do not use internal extraneous libraries which only offer a `double` interface.

Replacements of this type are generally only recommended for simple types. You must take into account the fact that the new type associated with the synonym will have to deal with the same operations as the original type. For this reason a class typedef is scarcely used or altered. The new class should have exactly the same methods as the old one.

You should also consider that your code will be more difficult for an outsider to understand if he cannot immediately see the actual type of a variable declaration. He will probably deduce the definition of `list` in the `list.h` file, but the meaning of `Book` will only become clear by referring to the typedef.

10.3.4   Unions

The significance of unions is much more limited to its compatibility with C than is the case with structs. They stem from a time when the memory space was more valuable that the programming effort.

Unions, like structs, are self defined types. They bundle several variables of other types. In contrast to structs, these variables cannot be used at the same time, but only alternately. All the elements in a union are filed in the same memory location. The size of a union corresponds to the size of its largest elements.

```
union NumberOrText {
  double number;
  char* textPtr;
};
```

Point notation is used for the different fields as in the case of a struct.

```
NumberOrText not;
zot.number= 1.33;
double number = zot.number;
```

The problem is that the compiler does not save any information about which alternative elements were allocated a value most recently. You can therefore immediately read out the pointer from the zot union which has just been allocated a number.

```
char* textPtr = zot.textPtr;  // Syntactically correct
```

This procedure is obviously risky. Unions provide a loophole for unchecked type conversions. Therefore you should only use unions if they are required as parameters for an integrated C interface or if you are programming so close to the system that every byte counts.

10.4 Type conversions

We have referred to type conversions in different sections of the book and would now like to consider them once again in context. We need to make a distinction between basic types and classes, look at predefined and self-defined conversions and discuss implicit and explicit casts. We will also have to deal with a number of different ways of writing these conversions.

Although type conversions can be classified in many different ways, our concern remains the same: the fear of a potential loss of information on the one hand and a desire for continuity in data transmission on the other.

10.4.1   Implicit conversion between basic types

You will tend to come into contact with implicit conversions between different types. You will anticipate one without consciously predicting it, as shown in this example of a conversion from float to double.

```
float source = 1.393;
double target = source;  // Implicit type conversion
```

This follows the assumption that the compiler will convert what it can. The different types will be directly allocated to each other. Although this appears to be a stopgap, implicit conversions have the advantage of making the compiler responsible for their accuracy. The latter can judge whether the conversion is harmless, as is the case here in the move from the imprecise `float` to the more precise `double`. If it is not harmless the compiler issues a warning or refuses it altogether.

This type of warning is an indication of a possible error source, which can be presented as follows:

```
char character = '3';
int number = character;   // Warning here
cout << "character" << character << endl;
cout << "number" << number << endl;
```

The warning is justified because the output does not correspond to what was expected

```
character 3
number 51
```

This is because we instructed the compiler to indicate the byte making up a `char` as `int`. Each character is stored as an ASCII value in the memory. The ASCII value for the character `'3'` is 51. This explains why the integral number output corresponds to his value. This type of confusion is typical of the interpretation problems which can arises during type conversion. Each type is associated with a whole range of functions and methods with which it is processed. If one type is converted to another, the same bytes are suddenly used by another set of instruments and may therefore be wrongly indicated.

Two further typical sources of error in conversions between simple types are high-loss conversions and conversions which disregard the sign. The former case occurs when a type with a broad range of values is converted into a type with a small range. This could occur, for example, when converting from `double` to `float` or from `long int` to `int`. The target type simply does not have sufficient memory space to accommodate the source type, which explains why value overflows occur. The latter case can occur when converting from `int` to `unsigned int` and is particularly undesirable because of its inconspicuousness.

In all these cases the compiler warns us of the possible consequences of using implicit type conversion. We therefore have time to consider whether we really want to convert the type in this way or whether it is too risky. You can use compiler flags to set the level of precision and detail required in the compiler's warnings. See Chapter 14, Section 14.3.

As we have already pointed out, the compiler can also refuse an implicit conversion if it is too risky. Implicit type conversions are generally limited to natural conversions between values in the broadest sense, for example from `bool` via `char` and `int` to `double`. Implicit conversion has its limitations however. For example, you cannot expect the content of a character field to be indicated as a floating point number without your assistance.

```
char* characterField = "London";
double number = *characterField;     // Does not compile!
```

10.4.2   Explicit conversion between basic types

Explicit type conversions make you responsible for their precision. The compiler conceals any warnings and follows your instructions. This can be expressed as follows:

```
double source = 1.393;
float target1 = (float) source;  // C style
float target2 = float (source);  // Classical C++ style
```

The first style is C style, which is as outdated as it is widespread. The target type is written in parentheses before the source variable. The second style should be seen as an analogy to a constructor call in classes even though it is used here for basic types. This style has exactly the same significance as the first but is only defined in the C++ standard.

Not only do explicit type conversions suppress any compiler warnings, they also allow for conversions between very different types. If you write an explicit type conversion, you should instruct the compiler to change the meaning of the bytes of the original type to correspond to the target type. This provides all the possibilities offered by implicit type conversions and more besides. This example shows what an explicit type conversion can do. It demonstrates the conversion from a character field to a floating point number referred to above.

```
char* characterField = "New York";
double number = (double) *characterField;
cout << number << endl;
```

We have converted a memory area of the size of a `double`, which begins at the point indicated by `character field`, into a `double`. Check the value that is given here for yourself. It does not have much in common with New York at any rate. Type conversions like this one only make sense if you can assume for a reason unknown to the compiler that the character string has been attributed a `double` meaning. This could be the case if you summarize a series of variables in a long character string, transmit this character string to another computer and convert it back at this point into separate variables.

Conversions between two basic type pointers can only be made using the explicit method. Pointer types provide information about the size of the listed variable. This in turn is important for pointers with field significance to enable the compiler to relocate an element. In addition when dynamic memory is released, the compiler must be notified of the size of the area to be released. And finally the type of a variable referred to by a pointer is just as relevant to the interpretation as a simple variable. It is clear therefore that conversions between different basic pointer types are too difficult to be dealt with by the compiler alone. Only you will know why the following instruction should be harmless.

```
double number = 1.234;
double* dPtr = &number;
int* iPtr = (int*) dPtr;
```

If you summarize the characteristics of the conversions between basic types referred to above to create guidelines, you will develop a multi-stage plan.

First of all you should try, wherever possible, to use the type that is expected in the particular situation. In this way you will avoid the main risks involved in type conversions. In cases where this is impractical, you can test the code with implicit conversions. If the compiler does not issue a warning, the conversion can remain as it is. Otherwise you should check to see whether the context of the situation is settling down. You can convert an `int`, which represents a shoe size, into a `short int` without hesitation. Implicit conversions, which are classified as harmless in this way, can be replaced by explicit ones. The remaining compiler warnings become more noticeable in this case. You should only use an explicit cast to make a conversion between completely different types in extremely specific cases.

> **Tip** You should avoid explicit conversions between different types, because they result in information losses and program crashes.

Enums can also be used as types in their own right. Because of their limited range of values, the compiler may expect an explicit cast in the conversion between `int` and enum. Otherwise you will be given a warning. Typedefs on the other hand behave in the same way as the type for which they represent a synonym in terms of their conversion capacity.

10.4.3 Conversions between classes

Conversions between non-basic types are never explicit and are therefore made by changing the meaning of bytes. This can be explained, among other things, by the fact that the C++ standard does not state how classes are represented by bytes in the memory. If we were to rely on assumptions about the memory layout, we would have no chance of porting our code to another platform or simply to another version of the same compiler.

Instead special methods are used for conversions between classes, known as constructors and cast operators, which can be called up implicitly. This does away with the messiness of conversions between basic types. Conversions between classes are no more risky than any other method call. No warnings will be issued for this reason.

Class A constructors can be used for type conversions from class B to class A if they use a single type B parameter. Cast operators allow for conversions in the same direction if they are class B methods and issue a class A value. Both variants are presented here in full.

First the conversion from B to A using the constructor.

```
class ClassB {};
class ClassA {
public:
  ClassA (ClassB b);
};
```

And a test to see whether it works.

```
  ClassB b;
  ClassA a = b;  // Implicit conversion
```

Then the same conversion using a cast operator.

```
class ClassB {
public:
  operator ClassA () const;
};
class ClassA {};
```

This works as well.

```
  ClassB b;
  ClassA a = b;  // Implicit conversion
```

You might be wondering why there are two ways of making the same conversion. One reason is clear if we try to replace the source or target of the type conversion with a basic type. We have already tested this many times with the `text` class.

```
Text = "Miles Davis";
```

The `char* text` constructor is used in this case. We will not be able to define a cast operator for the `Text` class for the `char*` type. After all `char*` is a basic type whose characteristics cannot be changed. For the same reason we are referred to a `Text` cast operator for the opposite conversion, which issues a `const char*`. It is therefore impossible to add a constructor with a `Text` argument to the basic `char*` character type. We have already implemented this operator

```
Text::operator const char* () const {...}
```

for the `text` class and used it for the output with `cout`.

```
Text text ("Kalmucks");
cout << text << endl;
```

We can see that both types of conversion method are justified if one of the types involved in the conversion is a basic type. The same requirements apply if one of the types comes from a class library that we did not write ourselves. In this case we cannot alter the type and must add methods to our own class for the conversion in both directions.

You should, however, be prepared for a loss of clarity in a conversion if a cast operator has been defined for the original class as well as a constructor for the target class for the same direction. The rules of precedent used by the compiler in this type of situation are so complicated that it is better to avoid them from the outset.

10.4.4   Dynamic type conversions

In certain cases it is not possible to decide whether type conversion is appropriate at the time of compilation. This is always the case when you want to convert a base class pointer or a base class reference into a pointer or reference in a class belonging to the same derivative tree. Let us consider two classes which are derived from the same base class.

```
class ClassA {};
class ClassB : public ClassA {
public:
  void methodB ();
};
class ClassC : public ClassA {
```

```
public:
  void methodC ();
};
```

It is extremely dangerous to attempt to make a conversion from `ClassA` to `ClassB` by actually changing the meaning of the bytes. Let us assume that you have access to a `ClassA` pointer, which you take to be indicating a `ClassB` object. You wish to call up a method which is defined only in `ClassB` and not in the base class `ClassA`. A direct call using the base class pointer is out of the question, as the compiler prevents this.

If you use an explicit cast to change the `ClassA` pointer into a `ClassB` pointer, you can get round this problem, but you will also have to undergo all the type tests. `MethodB` can be successfully called up if your assumptions were correct. Otherwise, the program will probably end, because you have changed the meaning of bytes which may be intended to describe a `ClassC` object to correspond to a `ClassB` object.

```
ClassA* classAPtr = ...;
ClassAPtr->methodB ();                 // Does not compile!
((ClassB*)ClassAPtr)->methodB ();  // Dangerous!
```

You can solve this problem in certain cases with the help of a `dynamic_cast`. This enables you to determine the type of object that is actually indicated by the pointer during run time. The base class must be associated with at least one virtual method in this case. Only then is the necessary type information available. A corresponding constellation which can be controlled using `dynamic_cast` can be presented as follows:

```
class ClassA {
public:
  virtual void methodA ();
};
class ClassB : public ClassA {
public:
  void methodB ();
};
```

You will now be able to access `methodB` using a `ClassA` pointer. If the object type indicated by the `ClassAPtr` is not appropriate, the `methodB` call will not be executed.

```
ClassA* ClassAPtr = ...;
ClassB* ClassBPtr = dynamic_cast< ClassB *> (ClassAPtr);
if (ClassBPtr != NULL) {
  ClassBPtr->methodB ();
}
```

Because the type recognition during runtime is rather demanding, you should use `dynamic_cast` economically. Chapter 7, Section 7.6.2 describes how `dynamic_cast` is a particularly useful tool in the case of multiple inheritance. With multiply inherited classes, the result can be NULL even if the base class pointer is present but not clear.

On the other hand, `dynamic_cast` only serves as a stopgap with downcasts as shown in the example, which should be avoided on a logical level. See Chapter 7, Section 7.2.3.

For information: it is always implicitly possible to reverse the conversion direction from a pointer indicating a derived class to a base class pointer. Every `ClassB` object is in fact a special `ClassA` object. You should therefore have no doubts about writing an assignment such as:

```
ClassAPtr = ClassBPtr;   // No problem
```

Pointers and references behave in more or less the same way with regard to polymorphous classes, or classes with virtual methods. Therefore `dynamic_cast` can also be used for references. The only difference is that no NULL value will be issued if the conversion is not possible. References cannot accept NULL values. This explains why `dynamic_cast` has to throw an exception in this case. Or in more specific terms, a `bad_cast` exception.

```
ClassA& ClassARef = ...;
try {
  ClassA& ClassBRef =
    dynamic_cast<ClassB &> (ClassARef);
  ClassBRef.methodB ();
}
catch (bad_cast exc) {
  // Error handling if necessary
}
```

This procedure makes it particularly clear that `dynamic_cast` should not be launched with random class references according to the scattering principle for the purpose of identifying the target type. Exceptions indicate the detection of genuine error situations and should only be used for this purpose because of their poor speed.

Conversions to the base class are also possible with references and are not associated with any risks. Neither of the two classes needs to contain virtual methods for this purpose.

```
ClassA& ClassARef = ClassBRef;   // No problem
```

10.4.5   Old conversions with a new look

You have probably already wondered why C++ defines so few keywords and instead continues to demand new sequences of brackets and special characters. Perhaps this particularity stems from the times when memory space was so limited that even codes had to be restricted. Does anyone remember?

It is difficult to describe specifically how a function declaration differs from a function call, a constructor call and a cast with all its variants. When typedefs are brought into play, it is no longer possible to identify what

```
knk (bbd);
```

means. For this reason, attempts were made in a later phase of the C++ standardization at least to clarify the significance of type conversions. The old cast styles could not be removed, however, for compatibility reasons. This means that three conversions with the same structure as `dynamic_cast` exist in addition to the type conversion in C style and the conversions in C++ constructor style. They are called `static_cast`, `reinterpret_cast` and `const_cast`. They do not offer any new functionalities. However, the clarity that they bring to the code should not be underestimated. Your difficulties may sometimes be caused by such a mundane problem as not being able to find a particular code location because you do not know what to look for.

Let us assume that you discover a conversion error in a large program. In order to correct it at all points, you will have to locate all the char* casts. Which search text to you want to use for your replacement tool? (char*)? In this case you will find all the function declarations with char*arguments, except in the places where you have included a blank character in the cast. The new conversion operators are easier to identify.

Whenever you want to convert between related basic types, you can use `static_cast`. This applies to situations in which an implicit cast issues a maximum of one warning but makes the conversion anyway.

```
double precise = 3032.56;
float lessPrecise = static_cast<float> (precise);
```

The last line has the same meaning as the following:

```
float lessPrecise = (float) precise;
```

Conversions between very different types are not authorized by `static_cast`. This is the task of the `reinterpret_cast`. The name indicates that this allows for the meaning of bytes to be changed. The example shows an arbitrary character string which is indicated as a number.

```
char* characterField = "Southport";
int number = reinterpret_cast<int> (*characterField);
```

The possibility of casting away the `const` of a variable has not yet been mentioned. This is the aim of `const_cast`. This may be necessary, for example, if you want to use a method written by a different programmer to which you only have access in compiled form.

```
void onlyoutput (char* textPtr);
```

You know that the methods do not alter your `char*` parameters, but your colleague has forgotten to clarify this in the form of a `const` addition. Using the `const_cast` you can still use the method for your own constant `char*`.

```
const char* textPtr = "XYZ";
onlyoutput (const_cast<char*> (textPtr));   // Compiles
```

The responsibility for ensuring that the content of `textPtr` is not changed is transferred to you via the `const_cast` from the compiler. You know that your program will end if, in spite of its harmless name, `onlyOutput` tries to change a text which is directly in code in quotation marks.

The name effect can be obtained with a C cast.

```
onlyOutput ((char*) textPtr);
```

Pointers in detail

Although pointers are not one of the preferred language elements because of their susceptibility to faults, there are nevertheless three distinct areas in which their use should be considered. Extraneous C interfaces which are incorporated in a program often use pointers as parameters and return values. Pointers are also required to indicate that an object or variable does not exist. They are also necessary to prompt memory space in a set which is only identified during run time.

This chapter deals with the first two of these three areas. The third has already been examined in the introductory chapter. A series of tips are also provided to help with the implementation of pointers. They also refer to the broader context of the subject.

11.1 Extraneous interfaces

The first area referred to in which pointers can be put to practical use is that of extraneous C interfaces which use pointers. Extraneous codes cannot alter them. Nor is this necessary if they have been thoroughly tested and have proved effective. If you are programming C++, you will have consciously chosen this language in order to benefit from the comprehensive existing C libraries and to make use of the homogeneous transition between a high-level programming language and machine-oriented codes. Many operating systems are written in C or at least use C interfaces. All these interfaces are just overflowing with pointers. If you want to integrate them in a code, you will obviously also use pointers.

If you intend to apply an extraneous C interface, you should first of all consult the corresponding documentation in detail to ascertain which memory you need to release. Pointers are a clear indication of a dynamically prompted memory, which tends to be released infrequently or at the wrong time. In the case of a genuine C interface, you must use `free` instead of `delete` if possible, but this too should be based on the documentation.

The next step is to get used to the return values and error codes which are typical of C logic. Because C does not recognize any exceptions which could inform the user of errors, this information tends to be concealed in return values. Methods or functions which issue pointers indicate an internal error via the return value NULL.

A typical function call which checks the return value for NULL and then uses it is presented below.

```
StructA* structAPtr = function1 ();
if (structAPtr != NULL) {
  // Normal program flow
  if (structAPtr->element1 == 10) {
    . . .
  }
}
else {
  // Error handling
}
```

A pointer indicating a struct is issued by the C function function1. Before we can read the value of a particular element of the struct, we must ensure that the struct pointer is not NULL. This can be checked in the if condition. Only then can we use a struct element safely. The same inquiry can be written in the following way using a simple trick.

```
StructA* structAPtr = function1 ();
if (structAPtr && structAPtr->element1 == 10) {
  . . .
}
```

The first half of the if inquiry checks the pointer. The NULL value is implicitly converted to 0, which is not an accurate representation of the actual value. Because C++ aborts when logical expressions are evaluated as soon as the value has been determined, structAPtr ->element1 will not be evaluated if structAPtr is already NULL. Two interrelated genuine values will be issued incorrectly if one of them is incorrect. This prevents an otherwise safe abnormal end from occurring. The entire condition will only be evaluated if structAPtr unequal is NULL. For this reason you must never reverse the sequence of the two conditions.

If you want to take things a step further, you can also include a method call in the inquiry. Because function2 issues a pointer on an object, we can execute one of its methods immediately. The if instruction does not require any other root.

```
ClassA* objPtr;
if (objPtr = function2 () && objPtr->method2 ());
```

This type of abbreviated style takes some getting used to, doesn't it?

Here we have tacitly presupposed that `method2` has a return value which is to be interpreted as a genuine value. Otherwise the compiler would not have authorized the method call as part of a logical expression, even if we had not been interested in the return value. We have thus created a link with C functions which do not issue pointers and which therefore do not indicate errors with a `NULL` return value. Because substitutions with pointer return values are preprogrammed, we need to examine these functions briefly even though they do not directly apply to pointers.

C functions without pointer return values generally issue `int` with almost the opposite semantics. The return value 0 signifies that no errors have occurred in the execution of the function. All other values indicate errors and are often shown in the form of error codes. The example illustrates the calling up of a C function with a whole-number return value.

```
if (function3 () != 0) {
  // Error handling
}
// Normal program flow
```

A call such as

```
if (function3 ()) {  // incorrect content!
  // Normal program flow
} else {
  // Error handling
}
```

which could be written analogous to a method call with a pointer return value has precisely the opposite effect. The return value 0 is interpreted as being incorrect as a logical value.

The entire error handling technique used by C is based on cascades of function calls with the error status embedded in the return values. The remains of this technique can still be seen in C++. If you declare a method or function whose return value is not indicated, it will automatically be `int` and not `void`, as you might expect.

```
function () {} // Return value is int!
```

This is a simplification of C notation in which it was understandably assumed that all methods which did not use a particular return value issued its error status. Therefore, for all methods or functions without return values, it is necessary to indicate the void explicitly.

```
void function () {} // No return value
```

11.2 Undirected references

The other application field in which pointers are irreplaceable is connected with one of their basic characteristics. Pointers must be used whenever references to objects and variables can be undirected or directed in a different way. References cannot achieve this and therefore also benefit from this feature.

11.2.1 Adding to reference strings

A useful example is that of a chained list, as already stated in a different context. All list elements have pointers indicating their predecessors and successors in the list.

```
class ListElement {
public:
  ListElement* predecessorPtr;
  ListElement* successorPtr;
  ...
};
```

Chained lists are such that they allow for the addition and removal of elements. To add a new element, the pointers of future adjacent lists objects and new elements are altered in such a way that they refer to each other. For the list elements predecessor, successor and new the code is as follows. The objects predecessor and successor are already in the list and new is added.

```
newElement.predecessorPtr = &predecessor;
predecessor.successorPtr = &newElement;
newElement.successorPtr = &successor;
successor.predecessorPtr = &newElement;
```

It is not possible to move pointers around in this way with references. References indicate the same object throughout their lifespan.

The fact that chained lists also require the object reference to be completely undirected is obvious if we consider the creation of the new object. This list element contains above all user data, which we have not included in the class definition for reasons of clarity. When new is generated, values are added to this user data.

At this point, we do not know the exact point in the list where the object will later be added. If we are dealing with a sorted list, this can only be clarified when the user data is known, because it has to be referred to for sorting purposes. The `new` references are undirected during the entire period when the object is being generated and up until it is added to the list.

11.2.2 Generating methods

A completely different situation, which also requires undirected references, occurs with methods which generate or consume objects. Methods which generate objects are so common that they have been given a special name. They are known as factory methods. They are always useful if you want to generate an object from a hierarch of similar objects in a program. You can indicate to the factory methods using a parameter which type you want to generate in a particular case. You will obtain an object of this type as a return value or, to put it more specifically, a pointer to this type of object.

Let us assume that you use a base class for file cards from which several classes are derived for slightly different file cards. The base class is called `Card` and the derived classes are `CardTypeA`, `CardTypeB` and `CardTypeC`. You can define an enum to enable you to name the derived classes more precisely.

```
enum CardType {
  typeA,
  typeB,
  typeC
};
```

An appropriate factory method uses this type as a parameter to generate the required object and issues a base class pointer.

```
Card* generateCard (CardType type) {
  Card* CardPtr = NULL;
  switch (type) {
    case typeA:
      CardPtr = new CardTypeA;
    break;
    case typeB:
      CardPtr = new CardTypeB;
    break;
    case typeC:
      CardPtr = new CardTypeC;
    break;
  }
  return CardPtr;
}
```

The `generate Card` method is typical of all other types of generating methods in that the object generation can fail. This is indicated by the return value NULL if the parameter contains an unexpected value.

Can you give me a type B file card please?

```
Card* CardPtr = generateCard (typeB);
```

Thank you. Remind me to remove it later on.

```
delete CardPtr;
```

11.2.3   Consuming methods

Consuming methods are given objects which are thereby transferred to the possession of the method. Possession in this sense means that the method is responsible for destroying the object when it is no longer required. This is noteworthy because this normally takes place in the part of the program which generated the object, i.e. the calling program. It is fairly easy to see why consuming methods are attributed to pointers. It is more difficult to explain why they have to consume. Why is a method forced to assimilate an object that has been transferred to it and why can this not be carried out with a simple copy?

Typical consuming methods are insert methods in list classes such as `List`, which has been referred to above. It is unquestionable that the list has the right to acquire the transferred object permanently. If you want to prevent all inserted objects from being copied before they have been included in the list, you must transfer them directly to the list's possession.

In many cases the consumed objects do not have access to an assignment operator or a copy constructor, which would allow them to be copied. This situation must not arise due to carelessness. Some objects must not be copied for technical reasons. We gave a number of examples of this in Chapter 8, Section 8.2.5 on the prevention of default implementation. Occasionally, consumed objects also have simple attributes of an extraneous class which does not have any copying methods.

As you can see, objects can be consumed for many reasons without the same applying to a copy. The way in which the object is consumed is obvious. Let us illustrate the procedure using the `List` class which possesses a

```
void insert (ListElement* elementPtr);
```

method. An object of the `ListElement` type, or one of its derived classes, is generated as `ListElement` is an abstract base class. It is generated dynamically using the `new` operator, because this is the only way the required memory can be transferred to the possession of another method. When the resulting element pointer has been transferred to the `insert` method, it is set at NULL. This puts paid to any temptation to reuse it. This final release of the pointer would not be possible with references.

```
ListElement* elementPtr = new XXXElement (...);
list.insert (elementPtr);
elementPtr = NULL;   // Undirected!
```

11.3 Pointers and const

We have placed so much importance on adding `const` to reference parameters that we should do the same with pointer parameters. The exchange method is presented below to clarify how we can change the variables of the calling program on the basis of a method using pointers.

```
void exchange (int* aPtr, int* bPtr) {
  int temp = *aPtr;
  *aPtr = *bPtr;
  *bPtr = temp;
}
```

They are called up from the superordinate program as follows:

```
int value1 = 10;
int value2 = 20;
exchange (&value1, &value2);
cout << value1 << value2 << endl;
```

This means that the same care needs to be taken with pointer parameters as with reference parameters. In contrast to reference parameters, it is possible with pointers to determine precisely when the associated object ceases to exist. It is generally set dynamically with `new` and removed if necessary with `delete`. It is therefore possible to use objects which are neither global nor attributes of a class as return values, as we have seen in the factory method example. A pointer used as a call parameter can also indicate that the object has changed owner. See `list::insert`.

Slightly different semantics have thus been established for pointer parameters from those used with reference parameters. Whilst with references you should take care not to change any objects which do not belong to the method in question, you should take the bull by the horns in the case of pointers. According to popular opinion, the element that changes the object should keep it. This can be expressed as follows in signatures with unprotected parameters.

```
void method1 (Object* objPtr);
Object* method2 ();
```

TAKE THAT!

The first method has the right to change the object referred to on the basis of the call. It is also responsible for removing it. The second method transfers the right to change the object and the obligation to release it to the calling program.

If a pointer parameter is labeled with `const`, it means that the associated object cannot be changed, as with `const` references. In this case, destructor objects obviously cannot be called up either. The object is therefore forced to remain in the possession of the same program section. The associated signatures are presented as follows:

```
void method3 (const Object* objPtr);
const Object* method4 ();
```

The first method gains read access to the object. It is later released from the calling program. The second method allows the calling program to consult the object. The class to which `method4` belongs releases the object at a certain point, at the latest in the destructor.

Tip Constant pointer parameters signify that the referenced object will not be changed and will not change owner.

Non-constant pointer parameters signify that the referenced object can be changed and will change owner.

You should bear in mind the fact that only the first of the two rules is supervised by the compiler. The second rule simply represents a convention with regard to the addition "and will change owner". Many programs observe the convention and therefore use the `const` addition to indicate possession conditions. Confusion occurs in programs in which two different parts change the same object that would have been the alternative. The above-mentioned convention therefore fulfils a natural need for logical consistency.

In order to be sure about the possession features of a

```
void method (Object* objPtr);
```

method, you should study the associated comments or, if they are not available, search for `delete` in the code. You may occasionally find an additional parameter which indicates whether the transferred object should change owner.

```
void method (Object* objPtr, bool consuming);
```

The call

```
method (objPtr, true);
```

signifies that the object has been transferred to the possession of the method. The call

```
method (objPtr, false);
```

signifies that the method has created a copy of the object which it can change at will. If you write a method with non-constant pointers you should always add a comment which removes all doubts surrounding the release duty.

```
// objPtr is released in the method
void method (Object* objPtr);
```

In the case of `const` pointers, you should also take into account the point at which the `const` is inserted. Pointers are defined to constant objects, as we have shown. However it is also possible to define constant pointers to changeable objects and even constant pointers to constant objects.

```
const Object* Ptr1;        // Pointer to constant object
Object* const Ptr2;        // Constant pointer
const Object* const Ptr3;  // Constant pointer to
                           // Constant object
```

There are a number of funny tips that can help you to identify the different sequences. Some advise you to read the declaration backwards in an almost satanic manner, while others separate everything to the left of the asterisk from everything to the right. But all you really need to do is follow the rule of thumb: do the same as for references.

References to constant objects are written as

```
const Object& ref = ...;
```

analogous to pointers to constant objects. Nothing else applies, as references always indicate the same point. Therefore constant pointers such as `Ptr2` and `Ptr3` are seldom useful. In practice they can usually be replaced by references. One of the few advantages of pointers is the fact that they can be altered.

11.4 Non-typed pointers

Among the different pointer types, the `void*` type plays a particular role. It represents the non-standardized pointer. In C++ there is no need to use this type, but it is required for compatibility with older C interfaces.

The reason why pointers are standardized is because it is the only way of transmitting the size of the referenced objects. This information may be required by field variables, for example. In addition, the principle of polymorphism can only be applied if at least the base class to which the pointer refers is known.

The explanation clarifies the fact that pointers whose underlying object type is unknown are practically useless. You can use void* to store any type of object but the object cannot be used from void*. Before you can do this, the pointer must first be explicitly transformed into a different type. A void pointer cannot be de-referenced.

```
Text* textPtr = new Text ("ABC");
void* voidPtr = static_cast<void*> (textPtr);
cout << *voidPtr << endl;            // Does not compile
cout << *(static_cast<text*> (voidPtr)) << endl;  // OK
```

The reconversion is only successful if the target type corresponds to the genuine type of the referenced variable.

```
(static_cast<Paar*> (voidPtr))->output (); // abnormal end
```

If a C function anticipates a void pointer as a parameter, it cannot do anything with it without assistance. Typically the same void pointer will be transferred back to the user who is aware of its type and can use it appropriately. This may be the case in the implementation of a chained list in which arbitrary variable types have been set. The associated functions can be presented as follows:

```
void appendElem (void*);
void* getElem ();
```

You should never use a void pointer unless you need to to provide a C function with parameters.

11.5 Function pointers

If methods could speak we could ask a

```
void read (const Text& x);
```

method to describe what it does all day long. The result might be as follows:

I read x.

The dummy x stands for the file to be read which is transferred as parameters. Whatever other methods we use in our survey, in most cases the parameters will be represented by dummies for nouns in the personal description. What do we need to do in order to parameterize verbs in the activity description? How should a useFile method look to do justice to the next description?

I do x the text.doc file and then I y-e it.

Function pointers provide the solution. The verbs x and y are transferred as function pointers xPtr and yPtr to useFile. The notation is rather complicated, as the function pointer type is indicated by the parameters and return value of the function. The parameter name used by the function is common to all signatures and irrelevant in this case. Let us assume that both x and y use a text as a parameter and do not have return values.

```
void useFile (void (*xPtr) (const Text&),
              void (*yPtr) (const Text&) )
{
  Text file ("text.doc");
  *xPtr (file);
  *yPtr (file);
}
```

Two more functions which possess the parameter list described need to be provided.

```
void amend (const Text& file) { ... }
void output (const Text& file) { ... }
```

By using these functions as parameters it is possible to call up the useFile. When the call is made, pointers are allocated to both functions. The parentheses after the function name can be left out as they are only required for the actual function call.

```
useFile (&amend, &output);
```

Tip Function pointers can be used to pass functions as parameters.

You may argue that the same effect can be obtained by transferring objects which have no attributes and only one method. Your argument is justified. It confirms the fact that methods are allocated internally to the associated class with the help of function pointers. When an object is transferred to a method, it contains data and functions. A hotchpotch of nouns and verbs are parameterized as soon as objects are transferred. Because objects are considerably easier to use than function pointers, the significance of the latter is reduced.

The standard C++ library uses huge carrier objects without attributes for methods. They are also referred to as function objects. Chapter 8, Section 8.1.3 gives an example of function objects and explains the general procedure whereby abstract algorithms can be entered in specific codes with their help.

TAKE THAT!

11.6 Safe pointer administration

It is enough to drive you mad! In long-running programs the memory is gradually depleted due to memory leaks. The program becomes slower and more voluminous and terminates when the main memory is completely depleted. This is all because we have been forced by unassigned semantics to use pointer variables and have forgotten to release one of them. In the automatic variables we have access to the perfect tool for tidying up the memory, but we cannot check whether they are idle. We need to find a way of equipping pointers with the same advantages as automatic variables!

No problem, we can do this. The hermaphrodite in question is known as an auto-pointer. An auto-pointer is not a fixed component of C++, but a self-made tool. For the `ClassX*` pointer type to be removed you need to write a `ClassXAPtr` help class. This uses a `ClassX` pointer as an attribute. All you need to do is release the attribute in the destructor.

```
class ClassXAPtr {
public:
  ClassXAPtr (ClassX* ptr) {
    aXPtr = ptr;
  }
  ~ClassXAPtr () {
    delete aXPtr;
  }
private:
  ClassX* aXPtr;
};
```

Whenever you want to use a `ClassX` pointer, you should generate a `ClassXAPtr` as an automatic variable at the same time. At the end of the block, the `ClassXAPtr` will be automatically removed and its destructor will therefore be called up. The referenced `ClassX` object will thus be removed at the same time.

```
{
  ClassX* xPtr = new ClassX;
  ClassXAPtr autoX (xPtr);
  // use xPtr
  ...
}  // autoX is removed and xPtr is released
```

Auto-pointers can be written in different variants, but they are all governed by the same principle. A dynamic object is allocated to the auto-pointer. Because it is used as an automatic variable, its destructor consistently tidies up for its charge even if the surrounding block has been terminated because of an exception.

> **Tip** Auto-pointers are help classes which allow for the release of dynamically set objects.

One of the disadvantages of auto-pointers is the fact that a different auto-pointer class has to be implemented for each pointer type or at least for each inheritance tree. However, this is not a problem if a template is used. The template is defined in the `<memory>` header of the standard library under the name `auto_ptr`.

Auto-pointers are a good way of dealing with memory leaks. They have been successfully used with many commercial applications and largely account for the latter's stability.

11.7 Avoiding duplicates

In times when memory space was scarce, it was important to be economical with the memory available. The task to be fulfilled by a program could generally not be changed. The indirect challenge was one of deciding which information had to be saved. The only way of getting round this dilemma is to avoid duplicating data as far as possible. The potential economy in this respect is huge. It is so easy to transfer the same data several times to any given method. In order to avoid abnormal ends, base low-level copies can be created in assignment operators and copy constructors. A number of copies of the same information are therefore created after a certain time. They are not actually necessary if they do not have to be changed independently of each other.

You need to sit down with a note pad and determine which copies are used for each object. You should then replace each different object with references to a central representative. This is how smart pointers work, they are not as difficult to use as the description first suggests. We have tested the procedure using a smart pointer which avoids duplicates of `Text` objects.

For this purpose we have written the `TextSPtr` class. `TextSPtr` operates in a similar way to a pointer, as a `TextSPtr` object is a reference to a `Text` object that is used via the `->`operator class. The trick is that several objects in the class indicate the same `Text` object and the same object counter via the `aText Ptr` and `aCopy Ptr` attributes. When the constructor is called up, a completely new text is created, whereas only another object's references are copied when the copy constructor is called up.

Let us begin with the constructor which exists in two variants. One awaits a `Text` parameter as a pointer. The pointer is to be transferred to the possession of the class and is therefore not declared as `const`. The constructor allocates the `aTextPtr` attribute to it. The constructor also allocates a counter which records how many `TextSPtr` the text is divided into. Because the counter should be identical for all `TextSPtr` which indicate the same text, it is also used as a pointer.

The other constructor variant uses a `TextSPtr` as an argument and is therefore a copy constructor. It creates a flat copy of the transferred object and raises the copy pointer by 1.

The purpose of the `aCopyPtr` attribute can be explained in relation to the destructor. The latter uses the copy counter to check whether there are any other references to the `Text` object. If not, it releases the object once again. This means that any number of `TextSPtr` objects can be contained within a `Text` object. As the copy counter is also used with a pointer, its value is identical for all the `TextSPtr` concerned. Their destructors can be called up in any sequence. As in real life, the last one turns the light off and releases the `Text` object.

At this point we need to explain how the user can implement a `TextSPtr` to access the `Text` object behind it. This is done using an overloaded `operator->` from the `TextSPtr` class. The `->` operator returns the `Text` pointer. This means that all the `text` methods can be called up without having to rewrite each one in `TextSPtr`.

```
class TextSPtr {
public:
  TextSPtr ()
    :aCopiesPtr (NULL),
     aTextPtr (0)
  {}
  TextSPtr (Text* textPtr)
    :aCopiesPtr (new int (1)),
     aTextPtr (textPtr)
  {}
  TextSPtr (const TextSPtr& textSPtr)
    :aCopiesPtr (textSPtr.aCopiesPtr),
     aTextPtr (textSPtr.aTextPtr)
  {
    (*aCopiesPtr)++;
  }
  ~TextSPtr () {
    if (--(*aCopiesPtr) < 1) {
      delete aCopiesPtr;
      delete aTextPtr;
    }
```

```
  }
  const Text* operator-> () {
    return aTextPtr;
  }
private:
  operator= (TextSPtr&) {}
  Text* aTextPtr;
  int* aCopyPtr;
};
```

The two different constructors can be used to determine precisely whether a new text needs to be created or whether another user simply needs to be allocated to an existing text. The former case applies if the constructor with a pointer argument is used. The foundations are laid for the creation of a new user group for the transferred object. If the copy constructor is called up, the user group increases by one and the `TextSPtr` object generated is simply an empty frame which refers to the actual text. Direct allocation is thus prevented by the fact that the allocation operator is declared as `private`.

`TextSPtr` objects should be set as automatic variables. This enables them to remove the referenced `Text` object as soon as the last associated `TextSPtr` is no longer required as reliably as an auto-pointer.

```
{
  TextSPtr textSPtr1 (new Text ("ABC"));
  {
    TextSPtr textSPtr2 (textSPtr1);
    textSPtr2->output ();
  }  // Reference counter decremented
}  // Text removed
```

You can also call up constructors in their copy constructor form, in which case the analogy between a `TextSPtr` and a `Text*` is even clearer. `TextSPtr` behaves like a smart pointer.

```
TextSPtr textSPtr1 = new Text ("ABC");
TextSPtr textSPtr2 = textSPtr1;
textSPtr2->output ();
```

The corresponding code with genuine `Text` pointers initially looks like this. It is only when the memory is cleaned up that the familiar problems emerge from which the smart pointer protects us.

```
Text* textPtr1 = new Text ("ABC");
TextSPtr textPtr2 = textPtr1;
textPtr2->output ();
delete textPtr1;  // Necessary!
```

```
delete textPtr2;   // Abnormal end!
```

You may have noticed something strange associated with the `output` call. We have defined the `TextSPtr` arrow operator in such a way that it returns `Text` pointers. If we replace the concealed operator call in the

```
textSPtr2->output ();
```

call by its return value, the following will occur.

```
(textSPtr2.aTextPtr)output ();   // Meaning?!?
```

This line is obviously meaningless, as the method name suddenly appears as a link behind the pointer without any other symbol. The evaluation rules of the -> operator protect against this eventuality. If an `operator>` is not called up in its predefined form with a pointer but as a user-defined class method, the result will be allocated an arrow symbol. The compiler first makes sense of this

```
(textSPtr2.aTextPtr)->output ();   // Makes sense
```

As the arrow operator has now been released on a pointer, `output` will be executed as planned.

We have created smart pointers as a means of avoiding duplicates of large objects. However a smart pointer also has a specific size. It has two pointer attributes and a copy of each one is created when a new smart pointer is added to a user group. This means that smart pointers are only useful if the referenced object clearly uses more memory than two pointers. Our `TextSPtr` will probably increase the memory space requirement of a program which administrates a list of contracted names. On the other hand, a server which supervises document exchanges in an office could be significantly reduced by a `TextSPtr`.

Object-oriented thought

By now you may be feeling overwhelmed by all the concepts, programming tricks, notations and user instructions with which you have been presented. It is now time to get rid of all the junk and simply concentrate on the main features.

We must make one thing clear: the quality of a program is not necessarily improved by using highly complex language elements. There are often many different ways of entering the same facts in a code. It can be very helpful to use the right trick at the right time. The decisions which determine the success or failure of the project as a whole do not concern syntactical subtleties, however. It is more important to ascertain whether you have divided the problem to be solved into different classes in an appropriate manner. If this is the case, you can easily replace a particular implementation by another one afterwards without disrupting the entire program.

If all the problems to be solved in programming are considered on a linear scale, the latter culminates on the one hand in the hardware and on the other in the abstract problem definition. The more technical the programming becomes, the more possibilities there will be to formalize the solutions. The nearer you get to the abstract end of the scale, the more you will be faced with the typical disorder of human thought. This applies to object-oriented design, which is therefore difficult to explain in the form of clear guidelines and is based more on experience and intuition.

Therefore we can only try, on the basis of a few typical examples, to formulate operating instructions which direct an untidy program towards the advantages of object-oriented logic. The feeling that you develop for the matter is just as important as the rules themselves. If you follow object-oriented logic, you will often be rewarded by sudden insights. From time to time you will say to yourself, "Wow, I planned that well in advance."

Because object-oriented design has become a scientific discipline in its own right, we also want to make you aware of its results. Towards the end of this chapter we will give a brief overview and references to the recognized procedures used in object-oriented design. Their quality and general validity are naturally quite different from the practical tips given previously.

12.1 Classes without attributes

A good indication that you are not exhausting the possibilities of object-oriented programming are classes without attributes. You enter a number of classes and after a few failed attempts the computer disposes of them. So in a sense there is no need for attributes, as the program can run without them. This is briefly represented in the following example.

```
class ConvertText {
public:
  void replaceUmlauts (Text& text);
  void removeBreaks (Text& text);
  void reIndent (Text& text);
};
```

The class has the task of changing text formats and removing distracting signs such as umlauts and line breaks. The procedure is as follows:

```
Text text ("Once upon a time... ");
ConvertText conv ();
conv.replaceUmlauts (text);
conv.removeBreaks (text);
conv.reIndent (text);
```

Now the question arises as to why the `ConvertText` class was required at all. It has access to a default constructor, a default assignment operator and a default copy constructor, but they are all unused and unusable. There are no attributes to be copied or allocated. The class itself is not used. The program has been written in a purely procedural manner with an object-oriented mask.

Class names derived from verbs are typical for this kind of dummy class. Verbs express actions and their meaning corresponds to methods and functions. The data forming the actual core of a particular class can be named more easily using nouns. If you take these aspects into account, you will see that the text to be formatted could serve as a class attribute.

A class can be reformulated in the following way:

```
class ConvertibleText {
public:
  ConvertibleText (const Text& text) {
    aText = text;
  }
```

```
  void replaceUmlauts ();
  void removeBreaks ();
  void reIndent ();
private:
  Text aText;
};
```

The constructor has been used here. It serves to initialize the aText attribute. This means that the parameters for the replaceUmlauts, removeBreaks and reIndent methods can be left out. Direct access is granted to aText. This process can make life much easier if a large number of method calls need to be made. In addition, data and the associated methods are located in the same place and the Text object is protected against data corruption. A text that has been transferred to the ConvertibleText class can only be manipulated by the three associated methods.

ConvertibleText can be used as follows:

```
Text text ("Once upon a time... ");
ConvertibleText conv (text);
cText.checkSpelling ();
cText.removeBreaks ();
cText.reIndent ();
```

However we have not mentioned the fact that you may also want to output a text that has been converted. Because of encapsulation, this is not possible. We can either use an output method for ConvertibleText or a getText method, which returns the encapsulated Text attribute. The former would amount to calling up the output method of the attribute, whilst the latter would involve an extra copy procedure. Neither solution is particularly attractive.

Now that we have come so far, we can see that ConvertibleText is a special form of a Text object. This relationship is expressed as public inheritance. In order to make the distinction, we have called the new class CText. CText is derived from Text. This means that we do not need to use a separate Text attribute.

```
class CText : public Text {
public:
  CText (const Text& text) {
    Text (text);
  }
  void checkSpelling ();
  void removeBreaks ();
  void reIndent ();
};
```

Now we can use all the methods which grant access to the `Text` class in addition to the new written methods.

```
CText conv ("Once upon a time... ");
CText.checkSpelling ();
CText.output ();
```

The lesson to be learnt from this example can be briefly formulated as follows:

Tip Convert the method parameters of classes without attributes into attributes.

In the second stage, we checked to see whether the new attribute could form a useful base class for our class. In Chapter 6 on inheritance, we explained why the inheritance of an attribute relationship should be favored in the case of specialization.

We do not want to give the impression that all classes should be given attributes in order to reach the only accessible path. There are examples of classes which do not use attributes and are nevertheless useful. Mathematical functions such as sines and cosines are often grouped together as static methods in classes which do not have specific attributes.

```
class Math {
public:
  static double sine (double x);
  static double cosine (double x);
  static double tangent (double x);
};
```

Objects in the `Math` class are never generated. Instead, their methods are called up like all static methods on the basis of the class name.

```
double y = Math::sine (1.3);
```

The only purpose of this class is to group the methods together and make the code position in which they are defined accessible. A globally defined `sine` function can be contained in any file, but the `sine` method of a `Math` class will probably be contained in a file called `math.h` or `math.cpp`. However, if we consider this more carefully, we will see that a namespace would suffice instead of a class for this purpose.

You may also wonder why the `sine` and `cosine` methods are not allocated to a decimal number object which is used instead of `double`. This is a good idea, but it would not be successful because the processors in our computers are optimized for operations with types such as `double`. The same operations would be less efficient in terms of scale with self-defined classes.

12.2 Methods with multiple parameters

Whilst the previous example highlighted how attributes can be used, we are now concerned with their numbers.

The `Image` class hosts a large signal buffer which can be represented in normal, mirrored or revolved format. The buffer is referenced with the `aImagePtr` attribute. In order to guarantee optimum clarity in the ownership relationships, the class creates a copy of the transferred memory area in the constructor with the help of the `memcpy` function. In this way each `Image` object can control its own buffer.

The class definition also highlights the fact that the methods have access to multiple parameters.

```
#include <string.h>
class Image {
public:
  Image (char* imagePtr, int size) {
    aImagePtr = new char[size];
    memcpy (aImagePtr, imagePtr, size);
    aSize = size;
  }
  ~Image () {
    delete[] aImagePtr;
  }
  void display (int x, int y, int color);
  void displayMirrored (int x, int y, int color);
  void displayRevolved
    (int x, int y, int color, int angle);
private:
  char* aImagePtr;
  int aSize;
};
```

Parameters which recur in several methods are good candidates for additional attributes. A more instinctive feeling is required in this situation. If too many of the parameters are made into attributes of the `Image` class, the efficiency of the program may be reduced simply from trying to tidy it up a little. This is shown in the following example, in which all the method parameters have been converted into attributes.

```
class Image {
  // ...
private:
  char* aImagePtr;
  int aSize;
  int aXcoordinate;
  int aYcoordinate;
  int aColor;
};
```

This arrangement may call for the creation of a large number of copies of the same image if you want to present it in different parts of the screen. An extra copy is required for each additional position because the associated attributes must be different. However, because the image buffer is the main element in the class from the point of view of data volume, it should not be copied too many times. This method is only really appropriate if you want to represent the same image several times in a particular position.

The color is quite a good attribute for an Image object as it tends to be a specific feature. The X and Y coordinates should not be left on their own simply because they do not logically correspond to the Image class. They can be grouped together in their own class. We have created the Pair class specifically for cases like this one.

After careful consideration, we therefore decided on this compromise in the creation of Image. The class has three attributes and their methods use one or two parameters.

```
class Image {
  Image (char* ImagePtr, int size, int color);
  ~Image ();
  void represent (const Pair& coordinate);
  void representMirrored (const Pair& coordinate);
  void representRevolved (
    const pair& coordinate, int angle);
private:
  char* aImagePtr;
  int aSize;
  int aColor;
};
```

It may be that one of the two useful methods is used later for coordinates so that a Coordinate class derived from Pair can be used to accommodate them.

The `Image` class can now be used fairly effortlessly.

```
Pair coor1 (410, 290);
Pair coor2 (300, 100);
Pair coor2 (100, 300);
Image monaLisa (bPtr, bLength, 3);
monaLisa.represent (coor1);
monaLisa.represent (coor2);
monaLisa.represent (coor3);
```

12.3 Methods with multiple return values

The suggested approach for methods with multiple return values is very useful and fairly accurate. The problems begin when more than one parameter cannot be returned directly. We have to authorize a transfer based on a reference which is not defined as being unalterable by a `const` addition.

Let us assume that you want to write a method that you can use to search for a person's address from the electronic telephone book. A solution for a method in the `Telephone book` class which provides this can be presented as follows:

```
bool getAddress (Text& street, Text& location,
                 Text& telephoneNo, const Text& person);
```

You enter an object which describes the person whose address you require and a series of void objects for the street, location and telephone number. If the person is included in the telephone book, the method issues `true` and the objects entered are associated with the corresponding values. A whole range of instructions have to be observed before and after the `tb` telephone book method is called up.

```
Text street;            // Void street
Text location;          // Void location
Text telephoneNo;       // Void telephone number
Text person ("Keith");
if (tb.getAddress (street, location, telephoneNo, person))
{
```

```
// street, location, telephoneNo are now filled
// enter values in own address book
}
```

This procedure is demanding and ambiguous. You have probably already considered grouping the return values together in the same class but have shied away from the task. In the initial stages you can simply use a class with the public attributes that we have already defined. We have also created an attribute for the person to make the procedure more complete. The aFilled attribute indicates whether the address is filled with useful values.

```
class Address {
public:
  Text aPerson;
  Text aStreet;
  Text aLocation;
  Text aTelephoneNo;
  bool aFilled;
};
```

With a method such as

```
Address getAddress (const Text& person);
```

or

```
const Address& getAddress (const Text& person);
```

the address search is made easier. The choice of which of the two signatures to use depends on how Telephone book is implemented. The reference variant is more appropriate if the addresses have been entered in a statistical list. If they are issued from a database each time a call is made and then disappear from the main memory, the first version should be used. However, the methods are used in exactly the same way in both cases.

```
Address keithsAddress = tb.getAddress ("Keith");
if (keithsAddress.aFilled) {
  // Add address to own address book
}
```

You will now immediately obtain a return value which contains the required address. You can also add the address as a whole to your personal address book and do not have to transfer each field separately.

> **Tip** If a method uses several return values in the form of references, you should combine them with a new object which acts as a genuine return value.

The new implementation method is admittedly quite impressive, but you might be wondering which object the `getAddress` method should belong to. Its task is to change the attributes of the `Address` object. It can do this easily, because the latter have been defined as `public`, but methods are intended above all to change attributes of the objects to which they belong.

It seems reasonable, therefore, to allocate the `getAddress` method to the `Address` class. In doing so we change the method name to `determine`, because this is more appropriate in the context. In order to protect the `Address` attributes against unwanted changes, we declare them `private`. They can still be accessed externally, however, by using specific `get` methods. The parameter which indicates whether the address could be determined once again becomes the return value of the `determine` method. It relates more to the process of searching for the address than the address itself.

```
class Address {
public:
  bool determine (const Text& person);
  const Text& getStreet  ();
  const Text& getLocation ();
  const Text& getTelephoneNo ();
private:
  Text aPerson;
  Text aStreet  ;
  Text aLocation;
  Text aTelephoneNo;
};
```

This new interface can be used quite simply to search for an address. The data is encapsulated correctly and the `determine` method is allocated to the address with which it is logically connected. An `Address` object can even be reused if a person has not been found.

```
Address address;
if (address.determine ("Keith")) {
  // Add address to separate address book
} else if (address.determine ("Susan")) {
  // Add address to separate address book
}
```

12

TAKE THAT!

The last relocation suggested for the `getAddress` method is to be recommended with some reservations. We have unilaterally optimized the interface so that the `Address` class is easy to use. Our starting point was the fact that the `Telephone book` object is available globally in a certain form and therefore does not have to be transferred to the `determine` method.

In addition, the `Telephone book` interface has been changed by the relocation and has probably not become more manageable in the process. If the only task of `Telephone book` were to determine how to provide addresses, optimization would be useful. The sometimes complex code used to determine addresses from the telephone book remains carefully encapsulated in the `determine` method and all the other program parts only use the `Address` class. However, if `Telephone book` authorizes a lot more inquiries, the method may be more appropriate for `Telephone book` for reasons of consistency.

12.4 Global variables

In our final style tip, we want to encourage you to stop using global variables. We might be going too far when we say stop using them, because we have not even explained how global variables are defined in C++. You have the option of declaring variables regardless of all the class definitions and regardless of the `main` function. The syntax is the same as with local variables. The only difference is their visibility. Global variables exist from the beginning to the end of the program execution and are visible throughout.

```
int number = 82344;
main () {
  cout << number << endl;  // OK
}
```

Because global variables initially appear to be very useful, there is a temptation to use them to solve all possible problems, but you soon lose sight of which parts of the program change which variables and how. Programs which use global variables are difficult to maintain. They cannot be incorporated in other programs which use global variables of the same name. They take up an unnecessary amount of memory space from the start of the program. Global variables are not encapsulated against unauthorized access. These lists could be extended at will. We must conclude that global variables are a Stone Age method.

We now need to explain how information that is to be used globally can be stored in a different way. Both namespaces and attributes need to be taken into account. An existing program library which collides with another because of a global variable can easily be made into a namespace.

TAKE THAT!

```
namespace MyLib {
  // Existing code
  int number = 82344;
  ...
}
```

The existing code remains consistent and executable. Only calls of your code from outside the new namespace have to be qualified with the appropriate name.

```
cout << MyLib::number << endl;
```

This prevents name collisions, but the variable has still not been incorporated in a satisfactory context in terms of content. If your library is too large, there may be a lot of areas that work with numbers. It is not immediately clear which one uses the above-mentioned global number for the namespace and which one simply uses a local variable of the same name.

The best thing to do, therefore, is to allocate the variable as a public static attribute to the class which is linked most closely to it.

```
class Telephone {
public:
  static int aNumber = 82344;
  ...
};
```

Each time the number is used, you can see which logical context it stems from and which file it is defined in. This also applies within a surrounding namespace.

```
cout << Telephone::aNumber << endl;
```

> **Tip** Shift global variables within a namespace or make them into static attributes of a class.

There is one more possibility: a programming trick known as Singleton is explained in Chapter 12, Section 12.6. Using this method you can create large global objects which are only instantiated when required, but which can only exist once at the most. However, you should not use the Singleton for a simple `int`.

12.5 UML

Using the instructions provided so far, you can pragmatically alter your programs so that they more or less correspond to the object-oriented structure of C++. You will benefit from this by improving the maintenance potential and clarity of the programs. You should progress slowly, however, and accept the support offered for rewriting or extending an existing program. We are assuming that the program is first written and then converted into object-oriented design. This is the correct approach in the initial stages, because you must first develop a feel for the object-oriented approach before you can sit down at the drawing board. You must make the typical mistakes in the beginning so that you can avoid them more easily in future.

But the demanding school of object-oriented design is not content with such incomplete work. It plans large-scale constructions on the same scale as an architect. It has developed a unified notation language for object-oriented design which corresponds to the well-defined symbols on a building plan. A group of design technicians, who are responsible for different planning aspects and complement one another, trade under the name of Unified Modeling Language (UML). They have created a de-facto standard for object-oriented design and make extensive use of development tools. In addition to program design, the UML also deals with the documentation of existing programs. Tools are also used in this area so that the complete circle of graphic structure diagrams can be automated back to structure diagrams via automatically generated codes. This is the only way of dealing with the iterative nature of software development.

Tip The UML consists of a collection of unified graphic notations which support object-oriented design.

The UML is a clear description language which is relatively easy to learn, but which cannot be explained adequately in a few pages. We therefore only intend to give you a brief impression of UML modeling so that you can assess the technique. You will then know which keywords to use to find further information if necessary.

The first and least specific step to be taken in project planning is to implement use cases. You will be able to use the two elements, actor and use case. A named communication relationship may exist between the two elements. Unconnected decision-makers and developers can use this very simple method to agree on which tasks a complex system needs to carry out.

Figure 12.1 *A simple use case*

It is also possible to identify business aims within the use cases and record the latter in box-diagrams with varying levels of detail, see Figures 12.1 and 12.2. A smooth conversion is made between natural language objects and object-oriented classes. If necessary, the class diagrams can also be allocated attributes and methods and static relationships can be highlighted between the different classes.

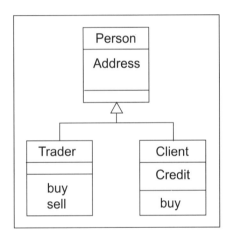

Figure 12.2 *Class diagrams for the same problem*

The dynamic behavior of classes can be represented in status conversion and sequence diagrams. Status conversion diagrams (see Figure 12.3) are useful when designing classes such as `File` in Chapter 13, Section 13.1 which require a specific operator sequence. Status conversion diagrams are also used as finite automata in addition to the UML.

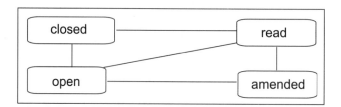

Figure 12.3 *Status diagrams in the file class*

Sequence diagrams (Figure 12.4) present interactions between different objects and take advantage of the fact that the control flow runs through a program in a linear form according to the context. Sequence diagrams are particularly useful with objects that interact strongly with one another. You may already have drawn this type of diagram intuitively yourself in order to clarify the call sequence in a client/server application.

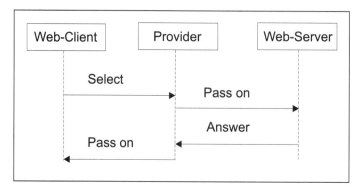

Figure 12.4 *Sequence diagrams for web access*

The UML provides a range of different diagram types and offers unified notation for the most common methods. This type of representation is not useful in all situations. Some diagram types have a trivial form for certain program types, whilst others soon become too detailed to be clear.

As you can see, the UML is not a magical solution, but is based on formal, healthy human understanding. Its merits lie essentially in its standardized representation of well-known facts and its independence from specific programming languages. It reaches its full potential when tools are used to automate the step between description and implementation in both directions.

As an addition to UML modeling, a large part of the worldwide OO community is involved in collecting design samples. Design samples offer elegant solutions for frequent programming problems. On the one hand, they differ from algorithms in that they offer object-oriented implementation instructions rather than handling instructions. On the other hand, design samples are different from modeling languages such as UML because they solve specific problems rather than simply providing descriptions.

A program's final code will never be totally generated by an UML tool. Modeling languages don't arrive at their level of detail under method and attribute names, whilst design samples contain specific suggestions for the implementation of given methods. However, what is far more important is the fact that modeling languages consider programs as a collection of classes in the form of building blocks which are only connected on the basis of the inheritance and aggregation structure. They simply need to be built up on top of each other to create a meaningful program. The content-based relationships between different objects are only highlighted by design samples which are more difficult to formalize because of these semantic components.

You have already been introduced to one design sample. In Chapter 3 on pointers, we referred to a factory method which generates objects from a special derived class irrespective of the enum parameters and returns them as base class pointers. This procedure is so common that it is used in many object-oriented languages and is considered one of the classic design samples. The decisive element in a design sample, however, is not its special implementation but its abstract, non-language dependent description of a particular problem and its solution. Design samples offer additional benefits in the form of unified conceptualization. When reference is made to a factory, developers can understand each other without having to refer laboriously to secondary requirements.

> **Tip** Design samples offer elegant solutions to typical programming problems.

Let us consider the procedure as a whole using the example of the Singleton design sample. The problem at issue is that of writing a class which can be instantiated on request, but for which only one copy exists throughout the entire program. It also has to be globally accessible.

In practice, this type of class could be required if a large object such as a parser is used in different parts of the program. Because of its size, we do not want to create a parser object in every parsed code section. A central parser can be used

TAKE THAT!

for all parts of the program. In addition to the size of the object, there may be logical reasons for creating it only once. A program usually only requires one object which creates a database connection, for example. Several connections would not only overstress the system resources, they would also create inconsistencies in the database. Both the parser and the database connection benefit from the fact that the aim of the Singleton method is to instantiate the object on request. If a program is not required to parse in a particular application, then you should not generate any parser objects.

The Singleton problem can be solved by writing the class with a private constructor. This allows you to control the object generation process. If the constructor is not public, it is not possible for every program section to generate an object in the class. So how can a class be instantiated if its constructor is private? Only you can call up the constructor, but the constructor is the first method of an object that is called up. A solution to the dilemma can be found in the form of a static method.

Static methods can be called up even if an object does not exist for the associated class. You simply need to write a static method which supervises the generation of the object. It controls a static pointer which indicates the copy of the class or has the value NULL if it has not yet been generated. The first time the static method is called up, the object is generated and presented as a pointer. For all subsequent calls, the object does not have to be recreated and only the pointer is presented. A program which calls up the static method can use the object and its public methods quite normally with the pointer.

In this case, a Singleton has been used for the parser example. The parser has access to a range of public methods. They have only been referred to briefly, however, as they are not significant for the Singleton principle. As you can see, the constructor has been declared private. The static method which supervises object generation is called getParser and the static attribute is aParserPtr. The interface definition in the parser.h file can therefore be presented as follows:

```
class Parser {
public:
  static Parser* getParser ();
  // Public parser methods
  ...
private:
  Parser ();
  static Parser* aParserPtr;
  // Private parser methods
  ...
};
```

The pointer attribute is initialized in the `parser.cpp` implementation file. In addition to the other methods, `getParser` is also implemented here in the form described.

```
Parser* Parser::aParserPtr = NULL;
Parser* Parser::getParser () {
  if (aParserPtr == NULL) {
    aParserPtr = new Parser;
  }
  return aParserPtr;
}
// Additional method definitions
...
```

The `Parser` class can be used in the following way in any part of the program.

```
Parser* parserPtr = Parser::getParser ();
parserPtr->init (regexp);
parserPtr->parse (text);
```

It might have taken you some time to discover this fairly tricky implementation procedure. If you keep the Singleton model and the scope of its application in mind, you will often find situations in which it can be used. Your programs will require less memory space as a result.

This is precisely the aim of design samples. You will have access to a whole range of clever tricks used by programming experts all over the world and will be able to pick out the appropriate ones to suit your needs. Because the semantic aspect is very important in design samples, it is not easy to formalize them. There are tools, however, which help you to use design samples automatically. In spite of this, they are still provided in books in the third millennium.

The standard library

The points indicated at the end of the first section have been confirmed in the main section of the book. C++ provides a range of constructors which serve to structure programs, but there are few commands which actually "do" anything. The core of the language can be likened to a versatile, robust skeleton. The actual muscles that drive the entire program are to be found at different points. You have the option of writing them yourself, but this often requires considerable effort. On the other hand, you can make use of a huge number of libraries in which you will find ready-made solutions to the different problems faced. C++ exists on the basis of these libraries.

This wide range of available libraries also has a disadvantage. Many libraries developed in response to a particular need and in a specific form. If you use a library successfully with computer architecture, you cannot guarantee that the same library will exist for different hardware or a different operating system. Whenever you are obliged to port your program, you should try to find a replacement for your favorite library. One will certainly exist, but the adaptation effort required may be enormous.

For this reason, the C++ standard has taken on a number of typical tasks and summarized their solutions in a standard library. All compilers claiming to be consistent with the standard must use this library. This guarantees that your code remains portable if it uses the so-called standard library. However, it also means that this library cannot contain any sections which are specific to certain operating systems. You will search in vain in the standard library for classes for graphic user interfaces, network communications or database access. However, it is so comprehensive that all its classes and template could fill an entire book.

We will concentrate on presenting the essential sections of the standard library and giving specific examples of their functions. This can only give you a foretaste, however. If you intend to do a lot of programming with C++, you should refer to more comprehensive documentation to find out exactly what the standard library has to offer. You will find that individual implementation becomes less frequent and you will tend to incorporate a class from the library. Not only does this make it easier for you to write the initial code, but you can also be sure that the classes from the standard library have been thoroughly tested and have undergone the manufacturer's compulsory maturity test.

13.1 Containers and algorithms

A significant part of the standard library is made up of lists in the broadest sense and algorithms which operate on them. For the reasons already explained in Chapter 9, Secton 9.3.5, lists of objects of various types are best implemented on the basis of templates. The standard library also uses this method and creates different lists – also known as containers – from templates. This explains why we use the term Standard Template Library (STL) to denote the part of the standard library referred to in this section.

13.1.1   Containers

The simplest type of container is the vector. It functions as a convenient one-dimensional field and takes over memory management, which is otherwise made more complex when fields are used. If you add the associated header file by

```
#include <vector>
```

to your program, you can generate a text vector as follows:

```
std::vector<Text> vText (2);  // Text vector size 2
```

Chapter 9 on templates explains how a special vector<text> class is instantiated, which uses Text objects as elements from the vector class template, for vectors of an undefined element type. A Text vector with the name vText is created at the same time.

Like the other elements in the standard library, vector is defined in the std namespace. It can be used with the prefix for the namespace or with a using instruction for its code without a prefix.

The Text vector can be used as follows.

```
vText[1] = "ABC";
vText.resize (4);              // Lengthen vector!
vText[3] = "XYZ";
for (int i=0; i<vText.size (); i++) {
   cout << ". " << vText[i] << endl;
}
```

Vectors are used in a similar way to fields. However, it is interesting to note that an exiting vector can be lengthened by `resize`. You will remember how complicated this is for normal fields. In addition, the length of the vector can be called up using the `size` method, which is not possible with fields.

The actual output is as follows:

```
.
. ABC
.
. XYZ
```

We can already formulate a basic rule for the use of STL templates. The classes that you used to instantiate templates should have access to the main constructors and operators. For example, the `vDate` object cannot be created, because the `Date` class does not have access to a constructor without parameters.

```
std::vector<Date> vDate (2);   // Does not compile!
```

Basic types can be used to demonstrate the capacities required of your classes. Allocation, comparison and copying generation correspond closely to requirements and there is a general tendency therefore to use them as variables. The creators of STL, for example, have used them in many cases.

In addition to simple vectors, there is a whole range of container templates which stand out due to one or more particular features. Although only the public interface is predefined by the standard, this often implies a specific implementation method with the associated run time behavior. The `list` template is therefore generally implemented as a chained list in reality. It is therefore considerably faster than `vector` when elements are added and removed. On the other hand, access to elements via an index is considerably slower.

Examples of other containers include `queue`, `stack` and `set`. They can all be added to your program using the header file of the same name. Queue is a line up, `stack` administers elements according to the "first in, last out" strategy and `set` represents a series of templates.

13.1.2   Iterators

Iterators can be considered as covers for different containers. They conceal the special features of a container type and thereby standardize access to the latter. This means that it is possible to formulate all kinds of algorithm on the basis of iterators without having to implement them separately for each list type. Iterators therefore create a link between containers and algorithms.

Not only does an iterator envelop the associated list, it also refers to a specific element. The ++ operator can be used to shift to another element and the * operator for de-referencing can be used to access the current element. The == equality operator for iterators is also clearly defined. Two iterators are considered equal if they refer to the same element in the same list. By combining these components, the vText vector can be output effortlessly from the previous section. The fixed iterators integrated in the container, which are accessed using the begin and end methods, are used for the initial and final loop conditions.

```
std::vector<Text>::iterator iText;
iText = vText.begin ();
while (iText != vText.end ()) {
    cout << ". " << *iText++ << endl;
}
```

The output is exactly the same as before. However, the difference is that we have not come into direct contact with the vector at any point and have nevertheless been able to manipulate it iText iterator.

Iterators come in different forms, depending on which operations you can and must carry out on the associated container. They are accordingly either well or poorly equipped with operators. An iterator that can pass through the container both ways may also understand the -- operator for an it iterator which cannot change the underlying list if the *it= expression is not defined.

13.1.3   Algorithms

The algorithms in the standard library can be used by a program on the basis of

```
#include <algorithm>
```

The basic idea behind the creation of this part of the STL was to provide the common algorithms in a form that was not dependent on the variable type used. A further aim was to limit implementation to the essential features of the algorithm and to give the developer as much freedom as necessary in terms of adapting to specific problems.

The first requirement is fulfilled by the sequence concept. A sequence is a section from a list which is described by an initial and final iterator. Because most algorithms are associated with lists in some form or another, the necessary data can be added to them in standardized form without it being necessary to identify the specific variable types associated with the list elements.

In this example we have used the find algorithm to search for the "ABC" text in the vText vector. A sequence consisting of existing initial and final iterators of vText is transferred as a parameter in addition to the required text.

```
Text abc ("ABC");
std::vector<Text>::iterator iABC =
  find (vText.begin(), vText.end(), abc);
if (iABC != vText.end()) {
  cout << abc << " has been found." << endl;
}
```

The second requirement necessary for the amount of freedom when using algorithms it fulfilled is the basis of function objects. Function objects are usually objects without attributes which serve as carriers for functions. In this respect, they are descendants of function pointers in terms of the language's history. An obvious advantage of function objects is that they are easier to use than function pointers. They can also use attributes if necessary, which maintain a status between two calls, which is not possible with function pointers. If a function object does not require attributes, its methods may also occasionally be defined as `static` and a function class is used.

So what does this mean in practice? First of all you can sort a container using the `sort` algorithm.

```
std::sort (vText.begin (), vText.end ());
```

However, if the sort sequence established by the inequality operator< of `Text` does not appear to be relevant, you can also give the algorithm a comparison function, which activates a new sort. This function is transferred to the sort algorithm as a function object.

```
Comparison comparison;  // Function object
std::sort (vText.begin (), vText.end (),comparison);
```

In this case, the class definition of `Comparison` must implement an `operator()` method which compares two `Text` objects. For demonstration purposes, we have only changed the sequence here. The list is sorted completely in reverse as a result. The new comparison function could be much more complicated, however.

```
class Comparison {
public:
  bool operator() (const Text& t1, const Text& t2) {
    return (t1>t2);  // Sequence reversed
  }
};
```

The other algorithms in STL can also be extended as required by function objects like `sort` in this example. In this case, only the abstract core of the algorithm remains unchanged and all the other elements can be adapted to suit particular requirements.

The STL contains approximately 60 algorithms in total. They are associated with a whole range of sort processes, set operations such as cutting and merging, searching for and changing list elements, and much more.

13.2 Strings

This is the moment of truth. We need to establish that we have written the `Text` class for nothing. The standard library contains the `string` type which controls everything that `Text` does and more. `string` is included using a header of the same name.

```
#include <string>
```

A string can be created and output at this point.

```
std::string string1 ("ABCD");
cout << "string1 is " << string1.data () << endl;
```

Another string can be added

```
string1 += "GHI";
```

or inserted

```
string1.insert (4,"EF");
```

two strings can be added together

```
std::string string2 ("JKL");
std::string string3 = string1 + string2;
```

or a partial string sought.

```
cout << "EF is in the position "
     << string3.find ("EF") << "contain." << endl;
```

Parts of the string can be replaced

```
string3.replace (3,3,"456");
```

and parts output.

```
cout << " Partial string " << string3.substr(3,3).data ()
     << endl;
```

Because `string` is defined as a template, strings can also be generated for character sets other than those represented by `char`. There are also iterators which can help to traverse strings and much more. If you deal frequently with texts, it is worth using `string` at any rate.

We have already come across two examples of streams: the output stream `cout` and `cerr`. `cout` is intended for normal outputs, whilst the `cerr` stream is used for error outputs. Another useful tool is the input stream `cin`. This can be used to allocate a value to variables which the user enters from the instruction line. All the characters up to the first line break are read in by the next lines from the standard entry. As soon as this has taken place, an attempt is made to indicate the characters as `int`. If this fails, `number` will be filled arbitrarily. Otherwise, `number` will be given the input value.

```
int number;
cin >> number;
```

As is the case with `cout` and `cerr`, you must also incorporate the necessary heading with

```
#include <iostream.h>
```

before you can use `cin`. This involves presenting the three named stream objects and a series of global operators called `>>` and `<<` with different argument types. For historical reasons, it is possible but not necessary to call up the standard stream with the prefix `std::`.

This is only a small section of the stream library, however, although it is the one that is most often used directly. The other headers also contain definitions of classes which serve the same purpose. They occupy a continuous data stream in portions in variables or chained variable values linked to a continuous data stream. The main differences occur in the form of the endpoint. For example, `fstream` contains stream definitions with a file endpoint, `sstream` is associated with string endpoints and even the name `iostream` is clearer if we are aware of this division.

The reason why these stream classes are made accessible to the user is because the second endpoint can also be different. The variables exchanged with a file or a data string via a stream can be of very different types. The necessary operators are defined for all the integrated types, but you will have to help your self-defined type to identify with the stream. You should define a method or function called `operator<<` or `operator>>` which uses a stream object and an object of your self-defined class as a parameter or return value.

The programming of stream operators is not altogether simple, because you will have to deal appropriately with the arbitrary character sequences that occur. Handling all the possible error situations which arise when communicating with a file is no easy task either. On the other hand, the benefits are enormous if this type of operator has already been provided. You will understand what we mean if you simply compare the convenience of `cout` with the C function `printf`!

13.4 Mathematical functions

Language elements for digital calculations must be included in all programming languages. C++ has a mathematical library which consists of four central parts. With

```
#include <cmath>
```

you can incorporate a series of functions which belong to the standard mathematical equipment. They include trigonometric functions, logarithmic functions, root functions, amount functions, etc. They operate on the basis of `double` values.

The `<valarray>` header contains the template of the same name for one-dimensional vectors. These vectors use methods for index access, element-based operations and vector operations. Classes for calculations with arbitrarily structured matrices are also included.

The instruction

```
#include <complex>
```

creates templates for different subsets of complex numbers. You can decide which typical basic number types will represent the two complex axes.

The `<numeric>` header defines a series of digital algorithms. They operate like STL algorithms on the basis of sequence arguments.

13.5 C standard library

Because C++ represents a surplus of C, the C++ standard library also represents a surplus of the C standard library. All the standard C headers such as `<string.h>` are also available in the `<cstring>` form. The first variant is identical to the C header and the second variant contains the same functions but as part of the `std` namespace. They can therefore be used with the same significance.

```
#include <string.h>
...
strcpy (aPtr, bPtr);
```

and

```
#include <cstring>
...
std::strcpy (aPtr, bPtr);
```

Most of the functions contained in these headers have become superfluous because of the more practical C++ pendant. This is the case, for example, for `printf` and the other I/O functions from `<cstdio>`. Only `<cstring>` and the above-mentioned `<cmath>` header are significant for reasons other than simply guaranteeing compatibility.

`<cstring>` hosts the functions required to operate `char*` strings. These include `strcpy` for copying, `strcat` for linking and `strcmp` for comparing strings. The length of a string can be obtained by using `strlen`. Although the `string` template is much more convenient, `char*` strings cannot be beaten in terms of efficiency.

Compilation

The other chapters of the book have not dealt with an aspect of C++ programming without which the language is nothing more than a useless convention, namely compilation. The prettiest code is worthless if you cannot use it to transpose an executable program.

This procedure is not part of the C++ standard, however, as the latter only establishes the syntax and semantics of the language. In order to encourage different manufacturers to compete for the best technical conversion, it leaves implementation completely open. You can thus find C++ compilers on the market which deal with compilation in very different ways. You even occasionally hear about C++ implementations which interpret the language rather than compiling it.

Nevertheless, over the years a typical implementation has become so well established that it should be explained. Compilers which differ from this standard implementation are either so convenient that they conceal all technical aspects from the user, or the differences are sufficiently documented for the compiler to be usable nevertheless.

We shall now examine the main contexts offered by one instruction line interface based on the example of the GNU compiler. Other compilers which can be operated from the instruction line may use different names for the same flags. In the case of DOS compilers, the flags are generally introduced with a slash (/) rather than a minus sign. Many graphic development environments also present the compilation process internally on instruction line calls in the manner discussed below.

14.1 Executable programs

The simplest way of generating an executable program is by calling up the form

```
c++ main.cpp
```

The `main.cpp` file must contain precisely one `main` function, which serves as the main program. It must also contain the complete definitions of all the classes used by the latter. It can be presented as follows:

```cpp
#include <iostream.h>
class ABC {
public:
  void method () {
    cout << "ABC::method executed." << endl;
  }
};
main () {
  ABC abc;
  abc.method ();
}
```

The result of the compilation process is an executable file which bears the name `a.out`. If you want to give the executable file a different name, you can do so with the following call:

```
c++ main.cpp -o prog
```

The executable file generated will then be called `prog` instead of `a.out`.

Programs which consist of a single file soon become confused. For this reason, the code is divided between several files for programs exceeding a certain size. In Part I, we discussed the division of classes between different interfaces and implementation files. For the purposes of our example, this can be carried out as follows:

File `abc.h`:

```cpp
class ABC {
public:
  void method ();
};
```

File `abc.cpp`:

```
#include <iostream.h>
#include "abc.h"
void ABC::method () {
  cout << "ABC:: method executed." << endl;
}
```

File `main.cpp`:

```
#include <iostream.h>
#include "abc.h"
main () {
  ABC abc;
  abc.method ();
}
```

Two steps are involved in combining these three files in an executable program. First of all, an object file is created from each of the two implementation files. Object files have the same name as the implementation file, but they end in `.o`.

```
c++ -c main.cpp abc.cpp
```

If the header file is in a different directory, you will also have to indicate its path using the `-I` parameter. In the next line, we assume that `abc.h` is situated in the `include` subdirectory of the current directory.

```
c++ -c main.cpp abc.cpp -I./include
```

The two files `main.o` and `abc.o` have now been generated. They can be combined with the executable program `prog` using the instruction

```
c++ -a main.o abc.o -o prog
```

It is also important at this point to ensure that precisely one `main` function is contained in all the object files concerned. In addition, none of the classes must be defined twice and all the classes used in a particular file must be defined in another one. This may seem obvious in this simple example, but it is not always as easy to implement in large programs.

14.2 Libraries

Let us assume that you have written a series of classes which you intend to use in different programs. In this case you can link each of their object files as described above with the different main programs to a different executable program. However, it is fairly difficult to keep sight of which object file is specifically required and which is superfluous. You have the option therefore of bundling all the object files that relate to a logical subject in a library.

Although a lot more classes are bundled in normal circumstances, we have only used this procedure for the exemplary class ABC. The result is a library called libabc.so.

```
c++ -c -shared abc.cpp -o libabc.so
```

We can now use this library and the tested main program to generate another executable file. The compiler is aware of the naming convention for libraries and concludes from the labc parameter that it should used the libabc.so library. The L parameter indicates the directory in which the library is located. In this case it is the current working directory.

```
c++ -a main.o -labc -o prog -L.
```

In contrast to the previous executable file prog this version no longer contains the class definition of ABC. Instead it is concerned with locating the libabc.so library during the run time. It then obtains the necessary information on ABC from the library. This may at first seem unnecessarily complex, but it has the advantage of allowing several programs running at the same time to share a copy of the library, thereby using less memory.

Another advantage of libraries is that they enable you to pass on your classes to a customer without revealing the implementation details. Libraries that contain well explained header files are a commercial asset in their own right.

Now that we have this background knowledge, the concept of the standard library is clearer. Even if we assume that a particular part of the standard library is represented by a header file such as <iostream.h>, this generally only contains the interface of the class. In reality, a compiler call such as

```
c++ main.cpp
```

contains the concealed addition -lstdc++, which incorporates a library called libstdc++.so the standard library. Only this enables the program to implement the standard classes.

14.3 Compiler flags

In addition to the compiler flags referred to so far, such as L and I, there are many more flags which influence the nature of the generated program.

The v flag stands for *verbose*. It causes the compiler to output highly specific information on which part of the compiler procedure it is implementing.

If the compiler is called up with the addition Wall, a number of warnings are issued. Warnings are indications of imperfect code positions and possible errors. Implicit type conversions which could cause losses can be terminated with a warning, for example.

You also have the option of optimizing the executable program so that it becomes very small and therefore rapid. On the other hand, you can instruct the compiler to retain as much information as possible so that the program can be examined more easily with a debugger. The former is carried out using the O2 flag and also includes inline optimization. A program translated in this way cannot be examined with the debugger. In order to make this possible, the g flag has to be used instead. The development version of a program is typically translated with -g, whereas the version that is provided to customers is compiled with O2.

The possibility of entering a preprocessor variable over a compiler flag is particularly useful. The D flag is used for this purpose. A compiler call with the addition DOS_UNIX has the same meaning, for example, as the line

```
#define OS_UNIX
```

in the program code. You can also enter the value of a preprocessor variable over the D flag. DOS_TYP=NT has the same effect as

```
#define OS_TYP NT
```

If you do this you do not need to touch the program code to impel the conditioned compilation in a particular direction.

Part III

Go ahead!

This part of the book is intended as a reference section for readers in a hurry. It includes a brief description of all the language resources referred to in this book. Special care is taken to ensure clarity and a schematic presentation, however, the different language elements are not necessarily described in a consecutive sequence.

Variables

C++ is very specific as far as variable types are concerned. A special type exists for every purpose and every size. The architecture of the computer and the specific meaning of a variable can be exploited to the full by choosing the correct type. The compiler carefully distinguishes between different types. Depending on the seriousness of the matter, unintentional conversion may be tolerated or may give rise to a warning or an error.

15.1.1   Number types

int

The most frequently used integral-number type. If you require a integral number and have no particular requirements in terms of its size, you can use `int`. `int` is signed. The value range of `int` is hardware-dependent but lies between that of `short int` and that of `long int`.

short int

Integral numbers with a small value range.

Value range: -32768 to 32767.

long int

Integral numbers with a broad value range.

Value range: -2147483648 to 2147483647.

unsigned short int

Integral numbers which only accepts values greater than or equal to 0.

Value range: 0 to 65535.

unsigned long int

Unsigned integral numbers with a broad value range.

Value range: 0 to 4294967295.

unsigned int

Unsigned integral numbers with a hardware-dependent value range similar to `int`.

double

Floating point number in the selection. Many digital libraries primarily use `double` as a parameter. All floating point numbers are signed.

Size: 4 bytes.

float

Floating point number with a small value range

Size: 2 bytes.

long double

Floating point number with a broad value range.

Size: 8 bytes.

15.1.2   Character types

signed char

Signed character.

unsigned char

Unsigned character.

char

The meaning is either the same as `char` or `unsigned char`. If you indicate `char` in letters, the usefulness of the sign is irrelevant. Letters are typically compared with each other or with constants such as `'a'` and are not associated with any arithmetical operations.

wchar_t

Maximum character set.

15.2 Self-defined types

Enums

Enumeration types or enums are used as clear ranges of values for numbers or other values without attributes. The compiler converts the different values into integral-number values. The enum ignores the significance of the number in the first example.

```
enum Color {
  red,
  green,
  blue
};
```

Colors can be used in the code like any other variable type.

```
Color eyeColor = blue;
```

It is also helpful to make use of the significance of the number of the enum value.

```
enum LinenType {
  pretty = 30,
  bright = 40,
  boiled = 95
};
```

If you do not enter specific numbers, they will be allocated to the enum values in ascending order. The first value is given the number 0.

Structs

Structs are used in C++ as bundles of variables or n-tuples. They may combine different types.

```
struct Person {
  int age;
  char* firstname;
  char* surname;
};
```

Here we see the declaration of a `Person` variable and access to its elements.

```
Person neighbor;
neighbor.age = 32;
neighbor.firstname = "John";
neighbor.surname = "Smith";
```

The potential of structs extends far beyond this example. In C++ structs have the same value as classes whose default attributes are `public`. They are hardly ever used in this capacity, however.

Fields

Fields group together several variables of the same type. Field variables have the same type as pointers on the first character in the field. A field of n elements of type `T` called `name` is defined by

```
T name[n];
```

A field of six integral numbers is therefore written as

```
int numberField[6];
```

The (`i+1`) th field element is accessed with `numberField [i]` and the numbering begins at 0.

Fields can be initialed as soon as they have been declared. They can be written in two different ways. In the first example, a field with three elements is created. The first two elements are initialized with the stated values.

```
int numberField[3] = {1, 2};
```

In the next example, only the initial values are given and the size of the field can be ascertained implicitly from their number.

```
int numberField[] = {1, 2, 3};
```

Multi-dimensional fields are declared by entering both dimensions in separate square brackets.

```
int field2D[10][7];
```

Typedefs

Typedefs are alternative names which are typically used for types which are otherwise difficult to write.

```
typedef unsigned short int sint;
sint number = 3;
typedef double Field5[5];
Field5 myField = {1.0, 2.0, 3.0, 4.0, 5.0};
```

Typedefs can also be used to standardize access to a type for a specific application requirement.

```
typedef int OdometerStandType;
```

If the `Odometer` objects used in your program are in danger of exceeding the value range of an `int`, you can replace the definition by another without having to change the rest of the code.

```
typedef long int OdometerStandType;
```

Unions

Unions are self-defined types which can behave like various different types. All the possible types are stored in the same memory location. The size of a union corresponds to the same of its largest element.

```
union NumberOrText {
  double number;
  char* textPtr;
};
```

The various fields are accessed using dot notation as with structs. The compiler does not check which type has actually been used.

```
NumberOrText not;
not.number = 1.33;
double number = not.number;
char* textPtr = not.textPtr;  // syntactically correct
```

15.3 Other types

bool

True value. This is represented by a number. `bool` is the result of a logical operation. The `true` value is a genuine value and `false` is an incorrect one. Conversions between numbers and true values are made implicitly. `true` is allocated the number 1 and `false` the number 0. Integral numbers not equal to 0 are indicated by all logical operators as `true`. Logical expressions formed from a combination of `bool` and `int` values also occur.

T*

Pointer type. For any T type, either self-defined or base, the associated pointer type can be created by adding a * symbol. The resulting type serves as a pointer for the memory area in which a type T variable is stored. The special pointer value NULL indicates that the pointer is undirected.

```
int number = 123;
int* numberPtr = &number;  // Pointer to int variable
```

T&

Reference type. For any T type, the associated reference type can be created by adding the & symbol. A reference is used as a dummy with the same meaning for a type T variable. References must be initialized when they are declared. They must not be undirected or directed in a different way. They are used mainly as method parameters.

```
double number = 12.34;
double& numberRef = number;  // Reference to int variable
```

void

Type without a type. In general void* is used in this context as a pointer to an unknown type. A void* cannot be dereferenced. The only way of accessing the referenced memory is by converting to a standardized pointer. void is also used as a return type for functions and methods which do not issue values.

```
void methods ();
```

void cannot be used in contexts other than the two referred to above. It is important to note that void type variables cannot be declared directly.

Classes

Classes are also self-defined types. However, they can be used in so many different ways that they will be dealt with in a separate section.

Numbers

Numbers can be noted as decimals,

```
413
```

hexadecimals such as the number 255,

```
0xFF
```

or octal numbers such as the number 9.

```
011
```

The variable type used for the number is affected by adding the character U for unsigned and L for long.

```
13UL
```

Floating point numbers are written with a decimal point.

```
3.1415
```

You can also use the exponential style, as we have done here with the number 5100.

```
5.1E2
```

Characters

Characters which are not represented by a specific symbol found on the keyboard are noted with a backslash \ and an additional visible character. The main characters in this category are the null byte

```
\0
```

the line break

```
\n
```

and the carriage return

```
\r
```

In addition, certain visible characters have to be masked by a preceding backslash because of their particular meaning in the string. This applies to the backslash itself

```
\\
```

the inverted comma

```
\'
```

and quotation marks.

```
\ "
```

Character literal constants in the program code are either used as a `char` variable value and enclosed in inverted commas

```
char nullByte = '\0';
```

or they form part of a `char*` character string. The latter is enclosed in quotation marks.

```
char* twolines = " line 1 \n line 2 \n";
```

15.5 Variable names

Variable names and names of self-defined types can be created from any combination of letters, figures and underline characters. However, they must not begin with a figure or correspond to a C++ keyword. The compiler distinguishes between variables using upper and lower case characters.

The following variable names are correct. The first two can exist alongside each other and refer to different variables.

```
MaxNumber
maxNumber
i
USER_NAME
line3
_PI_
```

The next two violate the rule on figures and keywords.

```
3p
while
```

15.6 Declaration and visibility

A `t` variable of type `T` is declared by

```
T t;
```

It is also possible to set an initial value at the same time as the variable declaration is made.

```
double number = 1.23;
```

Variables are only visible in the program block enclosed in curly brackets in which they are declared. Global variables are defined outside all blocks and are therefore visible everywhere. Variable names must be clearly indicated within their visibility range. If two variables of the same name are defined in a surrounding block and a surrounded block, the local definition will cover the global one.

```
int number = 1;                 // Global variable
main () {
  {
    int number = 2;
    {
      int number = 3;
      cout << number << endl;  // Output: 3
      int number = 4;          // Does not compile!
    }
    cout << number << endl;    // Output: 2
  }
  cout << number << endl;      // Output: 1
}
```

15.7 Constants

Variables can be marked as unchangeable by adding `const`. The compiler prevents values from being allocated to this type of variable. The value of `const` variables must be set when they are declared.

```
const int number = 11;
```

Because variables of any type can be declared as constant, this also applies to pointer variables. A distinction is made between constant pointers and pointers indicating constant variables – how contradictory!

```
int number = 3;
int* const ptr2 = &number;  // unchangeable pointer
const int* ptr1 = &number;  // unchangeable variable
const int* const ptr3 = &number; // both unchangeable
```

In a method or function header, the `const` addition in front of a variable indicates that it cannot be changed by the method or function. This is significant above all for reference parameters, as changes would also be made to the calling program.

```
void method (const Text& t) {
  // t can only be used in read-only format here
}
```

At the end of a method declaration, a `const` addition indicates that the method does not change the attributes of its class.

```
class XXX {
public:
  void method () const {
    // aXXX can only be used in read-only format here
  }
  int aXXX;
};
```

Operators

Operators are usually written as special characters such as +, -, * and /. They form inconspicuous links in the code, but possess a whole range of different meanings. C++ is particularly well equipped with operators, most have a predefined meaning for a few basic types. It is possible, however, to extend their meaning to self-defined classes. This makes operators interesting, because it allows you to extend the meaning of and redefine the language. Only the predefined meanings of operators are examined in the following list. You will find an example of a self-defined operator in the section on classes, see Chapter 18.

Arithmetical operators

Arithmetical operators are defined for all basic number types. Their meaning follows the sequence of addition, subtraction, multiplication, division and integral-number division, also known as modulo.

```
+, -, *, /, %
```

Signs for an X variable are noted as follows:

```
-X, +X
```

These operators have the meaning of pre-increment, pre-decrement, post-increment, post-decrement.

```
++X, --X, X++, X--
                \
```

This is simply a practical way of writing variables which are evaluated and changed in the same expression. For example, in this case the number variable is first increased by one and then output.

```
int number = 5;
cout << ++number << endl;  // Output is 6
```

The other three versions function accordingly, the difference being that the change occurs after the evaluation if the operators are situated to the right of the variables.

```
int number = 5;
cout << number++ << endl;   // Output is 5
```

Logical operators

Logical operators are significant for `bool` variables but can also be used with integral-number values, because the `bool` type entered the language range relatively late on. The meaning of the three logical operators follows the sequence of their name, and, or and negation.

```
&&, ||, !
```

They can be used as follows:

```
int n = ...;
bool nIsEven= ((n%2 == 0) && (n > 0))
```

Bit-by-bit operators

Logical operators must not be confused with operators for bit-by-bit logic. The latter carry out the operation in question separately with every bit in a number and the result forms a bit pattern. Their meaning follows the sequence of their name bit-by-bit and, bit-by-bit or and bit-by-bit exclusive or

```
&, |, ^
```

With bit-by-bit or, for example, all the bits set in the left or right operand can be determined.

```
int thirteen = 5 | 9;
```

The shift operators can be used to shift bits.

```
<<, >>
```

They have the effect of shifting the bit pattern revealing the number on the left by as many bits as are indicated by the number on the right. For example, a one shifted three places to the left is equal to 2^3, therefore 8.

```
int eight = 1 << 3;
```

The arrows indicate the direction of the shift.

Comparison operators

Comparison operators are defined for a large number of types. Their meaning is generally clear. There is a danger of falling into a trap, however, with the most frequently used comparison operator, the equality operator. It is written as a double equality operator rather than a single one. The `!=` operator stands for unequal.

```
>, >=, <, <=, ==, !=
```

Assignment operators

It is now clear what the simple equals sign is used for, namely for assignment purposes. The other assignment operators in this series

```
=,  *=,  /=,  %=,  +=,  -=,  <<=,  >>=,  &=,  ^=,  |=
```

are in the form of @=, where @ stands for a known two-figure operator. An expression in the form of

```
a @= b;
```

can be rewritten as

```
a = a @ b;
```

or

```
a = a @ (b);
```

if b is a compound expression. For example,

```
a += 3;
```

has the same meaning as

```
a = a + 3;
```

An assignment expression can function again as part of an expression.

```
a = b = c;
```

Pointer operators

The keywords and symbols used with pointers on an everyday basis are also operators.

```
*, &, new, delete, delete[], ->
```

The first two are used to de-reference a pointer and to determine a memory address.

```
int number = 10;
int* numberPtr1 = &number;  // & to determine an address
cout << * numberPtr1 << endl;  // * for dereferencing
```

The new operator serves to prompt memory during the program flow and delete releases the memory again.

```
double* numberPtr2 = new double (4.71);
delete numberPtr2;
```

Fields can also be dynamically promoted and released by using additional square brackets.

```
int* numberField = new int [3];
```

```
delete[] numberField;
```

The arrow operator allows you to use methods and attributes of an object which are referenced by a pointer.

```
Pair* pairPtr = new pair (1,2);
pairPtr->output ();
```

Type conversion operators

A range of operators exist for explicit conversions between different types. Their meanings overlap to an extent.

The standard C cast operator and its C++ pendant in the constructor style carry out various conversions on the shortest path. In doing so, they suppress all computer warnings and make the conversion in extreme cases so that the bytes of the original type are reinterpreted to correspond to bytes of the target type. Both operators are noted in pairs of brackets.

```
int number = 321;
char character1 = (char) number;   // Cstyle
char character2 = char (number);   // C++style
```

There is also a more moderate conversion operator which makes conversions between related types.

```
char* text = static_cast<char*> (Ptr without type);
```

This operator is responsible for changing the meaning of bytes, which is also controlled by the C cast.

```
char* characterField = "ABCDEFG";
int number = reinterpret_cast<int> *characterField;
```

The const feature of a variable can be changed with the C cast, but also as follows.

```
const char* constText = "ABCDEFG";
char* text = const_cast<char*> (constText);
```

The dynamic_cast requires an understanding of the class and inheritance concept. A pointer indicating a ClassA object can be converted by dynamic_cast in a secure manner into a pointer indicating a ClassB object from the same class structure. In this context, secure means that you can see from the result whether the conversion was successful during the run time. If it was not successful, the result is NULL. dynamic_cast can only be used for classes with virtual methods.

```
ClassA* classAPtr = ...;
ClassB* classBPtr =
  dynamic_cast<ClassB*> (classAPtr);
if (ClassBPtr != NULL) {
   ClassBPtr->methodB ();
}
```

dynamic_cast can also be used for references. A failed conversion is indicated by a bad_cast exception in this case.

```
ClassA& classARef = ...;
try {
  ClassB& classBRef =
    dynamic_cast<ClassB&> (classARef);
  ClassBRef.methodB ();
}
catch (bad_cast exc) {
  // Possible error handling
}
```

The other operators

There are a number of other operators which are difficult to group together. They include operators referred to at other points in the language description, such as dot operators for accessing methods in a class, the index operator for accessing a field element and the bracket operator for calling up methods.

```
., [], ()
```

There is also an operator

```
?:
```

which can be used to note an alternative in a particular expression. If the true value to the left of the question mark is true, then the entire expression is equal to the value between the question mark and the colon. Otherwise, it is equal to the value to the right of the colon. In this way the minimum of two numbers can be quickly determined, for example.

```
int minAB = (a<b)?a:b;
```

Precedence rules

The rules of precedence in the evaluation of operators are linked as much to arithmetical necessity as to the styles which can be used with a simple notation. In simple terms, we can say that operators which affect the language itself, such as casts and pointer operators, are evaluated first together with the one-figure operators. The subsequent sequence is as follows: arithmetical operators, comparison operators and bit-by-bit operators. Assignment operators come last.

However, you have the option of changing the evaluation sequence of an expression at any time by using brackets. The stated sequence has been reversed twice here.

```
-(x * (a - b))
```

Control flow

17.1 Conditions

Conditional instructions are introduced by `if`, the condition is given in parentheses and any necessary instructions are in a block.

```
if (number == 4) {
  cout << "The number is 4." << endl;
}
```

If only a single instruction has to be carried out conditionally, an instruction block is not necessary.

```
if (number == 4)
  cout << "The number is 4." << endl;
```

It is possible to give an alternative instruction or an alternative block, which should be carried out if the condition is not fulfilled.

```
if (number == 4) {
  cout << "The number is 4." << endl;
}
else {
  cout << "The number is not 4." << endl;
}
```

17.2 Multiple branches

Using the `switch` statement, it is possible to branch the required number of alternative values of a integral-number variable. The program flow will continue in the `case` line corresponding to the value of the stated number and will terminate with the next `break`. If no appropriate `case` line exists, the `default` line will be called up, if available.

```
switch (num) {
  case 1:
    cout << "One" << endl;
    break;
  case 2:
  case 3:
    cout << "Two or three" << endl;
    break;
  default:
    cout << "Not between one and three" << endl;
}
```

17.3 Loops

Loops can be introduced with the keyword `while`.

```
while (number < 10) {
  cout << number << endl;
  number++;
}
```

The condition can also be formulated at the end of the loop. This type of loop is generally traversed at least once.

```
do {
  cout << number++ << endl;
} while (number < 10);
```

In some situations, `for` loops are more appropriate because they contain the typical elements of a loop definition. They use separate sections for the initial allocation, the loop condition and the value alteration, which are separated by semicolons. Both the section for the initial allocation and the one for the value alteration after traversing the loop can consist of several instructions separated by commas. They may also be left empty. This loop outputs numbers from one to ten.

```
for (int number = 1; number < 10; number++) {
  cout << number << endl;
}
```

The following is an endless loop and an example of an absent initial allocation and value alteration instruction.

```
for (;true;);
```

Using the `break` instruction, it is possible to terminate the execution of a loop. The following loop is traversed five times.

```
for (int x = 40; ; x -= 10 ) {
   if (x < 0) break;
}
```

The `continue` instruction serves to skip a particular looping. The next loop outputs the numbers 1, 3 and 4.

```
for (int i = 1; i < 5; i++) {
   if (i == 2) continue;
   cout << i << endl;
}
```

Classes

Classes and objects

Classes are self-defined types which associate data and program codes with their particular uses. Copies of a class are referred to as objects. A class definition is introduced by the keyword `class`.

```
class A {
  // Class definitions
};
```

Methods and attributes

Classes can use several fields of different types. These fields are known as attributes. Classes can also include class-specific functions known as methods.

Using the keywords `private` and `public`, it is possible to divide a class definition into different areas whose methods and attributes possess private or public characteristics. Private means that they can only be called up within the class itself, whilst public methods and attributes can also be used for other parts of the program. If neither of these keywords is indicated, the elements in the class will be `private` by default.

```
class A {
public:
  void method ();
  int attribute1;
private:
  int attribute2;
};
```

An object's methods can be accessed on the basis of the object name.

```
A a;
a.attribute1 = 10;
a.method ();
```

18.1 Methods

Constructor

A constructor is a method with a particular meaning. It has the same name as the class and is called up implicitly when an object is generated. If a constructor uses parameters, they must be indicated when the object is generated. Constructors do not have return values.

```
class B {
public:
  B (int number) {  // Constructor
    aNumber = number;
  }
private:
  int aNumber;
}
...
B b (3);  // Object generation, implicit constructor calls
```

Copy constructor

Copy constructors are constructors whose only parameter is an object of the same class.

```
class B {
public:
  B (const B& b) {  // Copy constructor
    aNumber = b.aNumber;
  }
  ...
}
```

The call can be noted explicitly or implicitly by an assignment when the object is generated.

```
B b1 (5);
B b2 (b1);  // Explicit copy constructor call
B b3 = b1;  // Implicit copy constructor call
```

Destructor

A destructor is also a method with a particular meaning. It is called up implicitly when an object is removed. Its task is to release resources occupied by the object, such as dynamic memory. Its name is the same as the class name preceded by a tilde (~). Destructors have no parameters and no return value.

```
class C {
public:
  ...
  ~C () {  // Destructor
    delete[] aPtr;
  }
private:
  char* aPtr;
}
...
{
  C c ("Text");
}  // Implicit destructor call
```

Statistical methods

Statistical methods associated with a class can be called up irrespective of the existence of an object in the class. Statistical attributes can also be used regardless of the existence of the latter and occur precisely once for all the objects in the class.

```
class A {
public:
  static void method ();
  static int attribute;
};
A::method ();  // Statistical method call
A::attribute = 10; // Use of a statistical attribute
```

The initial value of a statistical attribute can only be set in the implementation file of a class in the following way. Initialization is compulsory, as is the case for constants.

```
int A::attribute = 13;
```

Overloaded methods

Overloaded methods are methods of the same class which have identical names but different parameter lists, such as methodA.

```
class A {
public:
  void methodA () {
    cout << "methodA without parameters" << endl;
  }
  void methodA (int number) {
    cout << "methodA with int parameter" << endl;
```

```
    }
}
```

They can exist alongside one another. The compiler decides which variants are to be executed when the call is made on the basis of the parameters given.

```
A a;
a.methodA ();       // Calling up the first variant
a.methodA (101);    // Calling up the second variant
```

Class operators

Class operators are special methods which, because of their analogy with basic operators, can be called up in a visible manner and are therefore self-definable. A `List` class, for example, which uses a `getLength` method could define an operator which compares the lengths of two lists.

```
bool List::operator< (const List& AnotherList) const {
    return (getLength() < AnotherList.getLength() );
}
```

This operator can be called up as follows for two list objects:

```
List list1 (...);
List list2 (...);
if (list1 < list2) {  // Operator call
    ...
}
```

Operators for classes can be implemented either by methods or by global functions. It is only possible to define class operators which also exist as operators for basic types. The possible parameters and return values of self-defined operators are given by the characteristics of the basic operators.

Default parameters

Methods can have default values for their parameters. The values are indicated in the method declaration by the equals sign after the parameter name.

```
void method (int number = 0);
```

The default value will be used if the parameter is left out when the call is made.

```
method (11);   // Normal call
method ();     // Call uses default parameter
```

Only the background (right) parameters of a method can be given default values.

Inline methods

Inline methods are brief methods which are optimized for translation. They are written in two parts in the header file and `inline` is added to the implementation section. This enables the compiler to replace any calls of this method type directly by the method root.

```
class Three {
  int getValue ();
};
inline int Three::getValue () {
  return 3;
}
```

this

Each class has an attribute with the name of `this`, which can only be accessed by the class is question. This attribute is a pointer indicating the object to which it belongs. The following class issues the value of `this`.

```
class ThisTest {
public:
  ThisTest* getThis () { return this; }
};
```

Two identical pointers are output when it is used in this way.

```
ThisTest tt;
cout << &tt << endl;
cout << tt.getThis () << endl;
```

18.2 Inheritance

Inheritance involves using all or some of the characteristics of an existing class when a new class is implemented. The class from which another class stems is referred to as the base class.

Public inheritance

When public inheritance is applied, both the interface and the implementation of the base class are inherited.

```
class A {  // Base class
};
class B : public A { // B inherits public from A
};
```

Initialization list

Using the initialization list, it is possible to initialize the attributes of the class and the constructor of a direct base class in constructors before the constructor's root has been executed.

If the base class does not have a constructor without parameters, this is the only way of attributing values to its constructor. Because an assignment in the initialization list affects an attribute in the same way as a copy constructor call, it is also possible to initialize `const` and reference attributes.

```
class B : public A {
public:
  B (int number1, int number2)
    : A (number1),        // Initialize Base class
      aNumber (number2)   // Initialize attribute
  {
    ...
  }
  ...
private:
  int aNumber;
};
```

Private inheritance

Private inheritance is used to inherit only the implementation of a class.

```
class A {  // Base class
};
class B : private A { // B inherits private from A
};
```

Abstract base classes

If you only want to inherit the interface of a class, you should use public inheritance and declare the base class as an abstract class. This means that at least one of its virtual methods will be marked as not implemented by the addition of `=0`. It is not possible to file objects of the abstract base class. For this to be possible with the derived class, all purely virtual or undefined methods of the base class would have to be defined.

```
class A {  // Abstract base class
public:
  virtual void method () = 0;
};
class B : public A { // B inherits public from A
```

```
public:
  virtual void method () {
    // Method definition
  }
};
```

Several classes can be derived from the same base class.

```
class A {              // Base class
};
class B : public A { // B inherits from A
};
class C : public A { // C also inherits from A
};
```

It is also possible to derive a class from several other classes. This procedure is known as multiple inheritance .

```
class A {  // First base class
};
class B {  // Second base class
};
class C : public A, public B {  // C inherits from A and B
};
```

Virtual basic classes

The addition of `virtual` when inheritance is carried out indicates that an object of a derived class should contain only one base class object. In the example below, an object of the D class has precisely one object of the virtual base class A.

```
class A {  // Base class
};
class B : public virtual A {     // Derived class
};
class C : public virtual A {     // Derived class
};
class D : public B, public C {  // D inherits from B and C
};
```

Overridden methods

In a derived class, a method from the base class can be given a new meaning. This is what is known as an overridden method. Overridden methods must correspond both in terms of the name and the parameter list.

```
class A {
public:
  void methodX ();   // Base class method
};
class B : public class A {
public:
  void methodX ();   // Overridden method
};
```

When an object of the class in question is stored, the associated method will be called up. This does not apply to calls made using a base class pointer.

```
A a;
a.methodX ();   // Class A method
B b;
b.methodX ();   // Class B method
```

Virtual methods

If a virtual method is overridden, the variant belonging to the derived class will also be called up when access is gained using a base class pointer.

```
class A {
public:
  virtual void methodX ();   // Base class method
};
class B : public class A {
public:
  virtual void methodX ();   // Overridden method
};
```

This type of call can be presented as follows:

```
A* a1Ptr = new A;
A* a2Ptr = new B;
a1Ptr->methodX ();   // Base class method
a2Ptr->methodX ();   // Derived class method
```

Protected methods and attributes

A derived class can access the methods and attributes of the base class which are declared as `public` or `protected`, but cannot access the `private` attributes.

```
class A {
public:
  int aPublic;
protected:
  int aProtected;
private:
  int aPrivate;
};
class B : public A {
public:
  void method () {
    aPublic = 1;      // OK
    aProtected = 2;   // OK
    // aPrivate is not accessible.
  }
};
```

Friend classes

Two classes which cannot stem from one another can nevertheless overcome object encapsulation with a `friend` identification. The class declared as `friend` can use the private attributes and methods of the other class.

```
class A {
friend class B;  // Friend declaration
private:
  int aPrivate;
};
class B {
public:
  void method () {
    A a;
    a.aPrivate = 5;  // Use the friend feature
  }
};
```

Additional language elements

19.1 Functions

Functions are known code sections which can be called up on the basis of their name. They are provided with parameters in the process and can issue return values. The definition of the `square` function is given below.

```
double square (double number) {
  return number*number  ;
}
```

It can be used as follows:

```
cout << square (1.42) << endl;
```

A pointer indicating the same function can be defined by

```
double (*fctPtr) (double) = square;
```

and can be called up by

```
double hundred = fctPtr (10.0);
```

19.2 Templates

Template classes

Template classes are class definitions in which a used type has been replaced by a dummy. A template only becomes a class when this type is indicated. Template classes are generally used as containers for other classes. The simple `container` template is typical in this respect. It incorporates an arbitrary variable type as an attribute and makes it available for read-only access using the `getObj` method.

```
template<class T> class container {
public:
  container (const T& obj) {
    aObj = obj;
```

```
    }
    const T& getObj () {
      return aObj;
    }
private:
  T aObj;
};
```

If you want to use a `container` for a particular type, you should use the template name together with this type in angle brackets as a new type. In the example, a `container` of whole numbers and a container of texts are used.

```
container<int> numberContainer (3) ;
cout << numberContainer.getObj ()<< endl;
container<Text> textContainer ("ABCDE");
cout << textContainer.getObj    ()<<    endl;
```

Template functions

Template functions resemble template classes in that one of the types required for their definition has been replaced by a dummy. In other respects they are structured like functions.

```
template<class T> void twoOutputs
  (const T& t1, const T& t2)
{
  cout << "Parameter 1 is " << t1 <<    endl;
  cout << "Parameter 2 is " << t2 <<    endl;
}
```

The type T must not be specified when they are called up if it obviously stems from the parameters.

```
twoOutputs (10, 20);              // T is int
twoOutputs ("Text 1", "Text 2");  // T is char*
```

Otherwise the type is indicated in angle brackets.

```
twoOutputs <double> (10, 10.2);
```

19.3 Namespaces

Namespaces make it possible to add a common prefix to any type, function or variable definitions.

```
namespace developer1 {
  class A {...};
}
```

Program sections which do not belong to the namespace must use the prefix in order to access its elements. The classes and functions within the namespace can call each other up without the prefix.

```
main () {
  developer1::A a;  // Store class A object
}
```

On the basis of the `using` directives, you can also render elements from a namespace usable by another without a prefix. This can be applied either to specific elements or an entire namespace.

```
namespace developer2 {
  using developer1::A;  // Class A usable without prefix
  A a; // store class A object
}
namespace developer3{
  // entire namespace usable without prefix
  using namespace developer1;
  A a; // store class A object
}
```

19.4 Exceptions

Exceptions serve to pass on error situations to a level in the program on which the errors can be handled. The exception concept includes the keywords `throw` for error messages and `try` and `catch` for error handling. The actual exceptions which provide information on the error type are arbitrary variable types.

As soon as an exception is thrown using `throw`, the program flow is interrupted and is resumed in the first `catch` block which corresponds to the exception type. If none are available in the method in question, one will be sought in the calling method.

```
try {
  ...
  if (error situation1) {
    throw int (999);   // Error code 999
  }
  if (error situation2) {
    throw char* ("error text");
  }
  ...
}
catch (int error) {
  // Handling of errors from situation 1
}
catch (char* error) {
  // Handling of errors from situation 2
}
catch (...) {   // The dots are C++ syntax!
  // Handling of errors of other types
}
```

19.5 Comments

Using the // sign, a comment can be introduced in the code which extends to the end of the line. Characters marked in this way are ignored in translation. They simply serve to enhance the clarity of the program.

```
int number = 4;   // This is a comment
```

Comments which extend over several lines can be limited by /* and */. This type of comment cannot be nested.

```
/* This comment begins in this line
and extends as far as this line. */
```

Preprocessor instructions

The preprocessor is responsible for altering the program code before it is translated by the compiler. Instructions for the preprocessor are identified by an initial double cross and stand at the beginning of the line.

Includes

The `include` instruction serves to integrate header files required for the translation into the code. This can take place with two variables. Self-made headers are given in quotation marks, whilst standard library headers are given in angle brackets.

```
#include "pair.h"      // Own header
#include <iostream.h>   // Standard library header
```

Macros

Macros are instructions for text replacements in the code. With the following macro, MY_NUMBERTYPE will be replaced by double in the code each time it occurs.

```
#define MY_NUMBERTYPE double
```

Macros can also use parameters, as shown in this example, which form the square of a value.

```
#define SQUARE(x) x*x
```

The parameter can be placed in quotation marks with a double cross followed by the parameter name within the replacement expression. Line breaks must be marked with a backslash (\).

```
#define SQUARE (x) \
cout << #x " squared is " <<  x*x << endl;
```

The output of

```
SQUARE (3)
```

is

```
3 squared is 9
```

Two double crosses in macro definitions are used to mark consecutive parameters. The impulsive instructions

```
#define XXX(a,b) a##b << " Hello " << endl;
XXX(co,ut)
```

have the same effect as the line

```
cout << " Hello " << endl;
```

Because macros only operate on the level of text replacement without carrying out syntactical checks, they are not type safe and are extremely error prone.

Conditional translation

However, macros can also be used in an attenuated form to allow for conditional compilation. If, for example, the line

```
#define TEST_VERSION
```

appears at the beginning of the source file, a simple version of the program will be created when the compiling process is carried out. Otherwise, a full-function program version will be created.

```
#ifdef TEST_VERSION
...  // Simplified code
#else
...  // Full-function code
#endif
```

By using

```
#undef TEST_VERSION
```

you can remove a preprocessor variable that has already been used.

The preprocessor instructions `#if Expression` and `#elif Expression` can be combined with `#else` and `#endif` if the expression works out as 0 or a whole number not equal to 0.

Code of the text class

The Text class, which is gradually expanded as the book progresses, is listed here in full. The addition operator is the variant which is used as a global function.

file text.h:

```
class Text {
public:

  // Friend declaration for the addition function
  friend Text operator+ (const text& , const text& );

  // Constructor with C string argument
  Text (const char* textPtr);

  // Parameterless constructor
  // As implicit inline method
  Text () : aTextPtr (NULL) {;}

  // Copy constructor
  Text (const text& text);

  // Destructor
  ~Text ();

  // Relational operator
  bool operator== (const Text& text) const;

  // Index operator
  char operator[] (int index) const;

  // Method for determining length
```

```cpp
    int getLength () const;

    // Cast operator to C string
    operator const char*() const;

    // Assignment operator
    const Text& operator= (const Text& text);

    // Method for displaying text
    void output () const ;

private:
    // Pointer attribute, points to the text
    char* aTextPtr;
};

// Addition operator as global function
Text operator+ (const text& ls, const text& rs);
```

file text.cpp:

```cpp
#include <iostream.h>  // For cout
#include <string.h>  // For strcpy, strcmp, strlen
#include "text.h"

// Constructor with C string argument
Text::Text (const char* textPtr) : aTextPtr (NULL) {
  if (textPtr != NULL) {
    aTextPtr = new char [strlen(textPtr) +1];
    strcpy (aTextPtr, textPtr);
  }
}

// Copy constructor
Text::Text (const Text& text) : aTextPtr (NULL) {
  if (text.aTextPtr != NULL) {
    aTextPtr = new char[strlen (text.aTextPtr)+1];
    strcpy (aTextPtr, text.aTextPtr);
  }
}

// Destructor
```

```
Text::~Text () {
  delete[] aTextPtr;
}

// Relational operator
bool Text::operator== (const Text& text) const {
  if (aTextPtr == NULL || text.aTextPtr == NULL) {
    return (aTextPtr == NULL && text.aTextPtr == NULL);
  }
  return (strcmp (aTextPtr, text.aTextPtr) == 0);
}

// Index operator
char Text::operator[] (int index) const {
  if (0 <= index && index < getLength() ) {
    return aTextPtr[index];
  }
  else {
    return '\0';
  }
}

// Method for determining length of text
int Text::getLength () const {
  if (aTextPtr == NULL) {
     return 0;
  } else {
    return strlen (aTextPtr);
  }
}

// Cast operator to C string
Text::operator const char*() const {
  return aTextPtr;
}

// Assignment operator
const Text& Text::operator= (const Text& text) {
  // avoid self-assignment
  if (this == &text) {
    return *this;
  }
```

```cpp
    // Normal assignment
    delete[] aTextPtr;
    if (text.aTextPtr != NULL) {
      aTextPtr = new char[strlen (text.aTextPtr) +1];
      strcpy (aTextPtr, text.aTextPtr);
    } else {
      // NULL assignment
      aTextPtr = NULL;
    }
    return *this;
}

// Output method
void Text::output () const {
  cout << aTextPtr << endl;
}

// Addition operator
Text operator+ (const Text& ls, const Text& rs) {
  Text ret;
  // The two addends are not empty
  if (ls.aTextPtr != NULL && rs.aTextPtr != NULL) {
    ret.aTextPtr = new char
      [strlen(ls.aTextPtr) + strlen(rs.aTextPtr) +1];
    strcpy (ret.aTextPtr, ls.aTextPtr);
    strcat (ret.aTextPtr, rs.aTextPtr);
  // Right-hand addend only and not empty
  } else if (rs.aTextPtr != NULL) {
    ret = rs;
  // Left-hand addend only and not empty
  } else if (ls.aTextPtr != NULL) {
    ret = ls;
  }
  return ret;
}
```

A

Index